PAUL
POIRET

Alice Mackrell

Holmes & Meier · New York

To the memory of my parents
Julia and William McKay

Frontispiece: Madame Poiret, Gouache by Georges
Lepape, 1911
(Courtauld Institute of Art, London)

Published in the United States of America 1990 by
Holmes & Meier Publishers, Inc.
30 Irving Place
New York, NY 10003

First published 1990

Library of Congress Cataloging-in-Publication Data

Mackrell, Alice.
    Paul Poiret/Alice Mackrell.
        p.   cm. — (Fashion designers)
    Includes bibliographical references.
    ISBN 0-8419-1279-3. — ISBN 0-8419-1280-7
    (pbk.)
    1. Costume design — France — History —
20th century. 2. Costume designers —
France.   3. Poiret, Paul.   I. Title.   II. Series.
TT507.M346 1990   90-4086
746.9′2′092—dc20   CIP

Filmset by Lasertext Ltd., Thomas Street, Stretford,
Manchester

and printed in Great Britain by
The Bath Press, Avon

4·95

PAUL
POIRET

CONTENTS

ACKNOWLEDGEMENTS

I would like to offer my thanks to the people who have helped me in the preparation of this book: Dr Aileen Ribeiro of the History of Dress Department, Courtauld Institute of Art, London; Miss Rachel Wright, Miss Pauline Snelson and Mrs Clare Sunderland of B. T. Batsford; Miss Penelope Byrde of the Museum of Costume, Bath; Madame Marie-Dominique Frieh and Madame Monique Jay of the Musée Historique des Tissus, Lyons; and Miss Kerry Taylor of the Collectors' Department, Sotheby's, London. Finally, my special thanks to my brother, Charles McKay, for once again sending me so many useful books from America.

LIST OF ILLUSTRATIONS

LIST OF COLOUR PLATES

(between pages 48 and 49)

INTRODUCTION

In his autobiography, *My First Fifty Years*, Poiret asked:

> '*Am I a fool when I dream of putting art into my dresses, a fool when I say dressmaking is an art.*[1] ... *For I have always loved painters, and felt on an equal footing with them. It seems to me that we practise the same craft and that they are my fellow workers.*[2]

Poiret was also the first couturier to relate fashion successfully to the other arts. Fashion illustration was one of the major areas into which he imbued new life with the help of artists. In late eighteenth- and early nineteenth-century France, fashion illustration had reached a very high standard through the fashion plates of the *Journal des Dames et des Modes*. However, as the nineteenth century progressed, fashion illustration degenerated, with the closure of the *Journal des Dames et des Modes* in 1839 and the invention of photography.[3] The *Journal des Dames et des Modes* had been founded in 1797 by Pierre de La Mésangère. It was the first fashion magazine in which the clothes depicted in the fashion plates were sketched from life and the models easily recognized by those who moved in the *beau monde*. The plates were noted for their accuracy and aestheticism and for the way that they directly related dress to fashionable society through the use of settings such as the gardens of Frascati and Tivoli, where the élite gathered, or empty backgrounds with just a piece of period furniture (figs. 1 and 2). Moreover, they were drawn by a small group of artists who were outstanding draughtsmen and faithful social chroniclers; men such as Philibert-Louis Debucourt and Horace and Carle Vernet.[4]

Poiret's originality lay in recognizing the need for a rejuvenation of fashion illustration along the lines of the *Journal des Dames et des Modes*. He was innovative in commissioning one artist for one album of fashion drawings. In 1908, having been established in his own fashion house for a mere five years, Poiret commissioned Paul Iribe to produce *Les robes de Paul Poiret racontées par Paul Iribe*. This album was so successful that it was followed in 1911 by *Les choses de Paul Poiret vues par Georges Lepape*. The importance accorded to the artists is immediately recognizable in the titles of the works – the gowns of Paul Poiret 'as

1 and 2 **Fashion plates from the**
Journal des Dames et des Modes
for 18 July 1799 and 22 October 1799.
This periodical is the primary
source for studying French fashions
of the Directoire, the distinctive
style of dress associated with
the period 1795–9, characterized
by gowns with high waistlines
and long, straight skirts.

related' by Paul Iribe, and the things of Paul Poiret 'as seen' by Georges Lepape.

Paul Iribe was an artist who was also a fashion designer and interior decorator. He was a very subtle draughtsman and created, edited and illustrated the witty, avant-garde magazine *Le Témoin*. *Les robes de Paul Poiret racontées par Paul Iribe*, a collection of ten illustrations, was a work of great simplicity and clarity, reflecting Poiret's interpretation of the neo-classical style of dress of late eighteenth-century France – long and straight and with a high waistline.

Dress reformers in the 1880s, and again in the 1900s, had advocated the liberation of the body and the adoption of the classical-style high waistline, and fashion plates show some experimentation with this silhouette. However, it was Poiret, more than any other couturier, who most successfully developed and refined the neo-classical line and promoted it through the kind of fashion illustration it deserved. Some contemporary designers felt very much under threat. For example, when Poiret joined La Maison Worth in 1901, it was directed by the great couturier's sons, Gaston and Jean. Poiret sensed that Jean foresaw what lay ahead for Jean later came to call Poiret's neo-classical creations 'dishcloths'.

> *M. Jean Worth was not very pleased at having introduced into his House an element which, in his opinion lowered it. He did not like me very much, because in his eyes I represented a new spirit, in which there was a force (he felt it) which was to destroy and sweep away all his dreams.*[5]

Directoire Revival was the term used in France to describe dress based on the neo-classical line and the title of the illustration shown here, drawn by Iribe, is called 'Trois robes Directoire' (fig. 3). The Directoire was the period of government in France from 1795 to 1799. Neo-classicism was the artistic movement of that era and included

3   Three Directoire gowns by Paul Poiret. From Les robes de Paul Poiret racontées par Paul Iribe, *1908. Iribe has grouped the figures in a Directoire interior, experimenting with the technique of leaving a large area of the background unfilled and thus showing the high quality of the handmade paper, a technique reminiscent of the fashion plates of the Directoire. The Poiret gowns are very simple with the skirt long and tubular in shape and the waistline high, recalling the neo-classical style of the Directoire. Colours are plain, clear and bold. Very small geometrical designs were also fashionable. The mannequins also suggest the Directoire with their short hair in loose curls set off by Grecian-style fillets.*

4 **'The cushions'** from *Les choses de Paul Poiret vues par Georges Lepape*, **1911. Lepape presents one of his favourite themes, a fashionable lady stretched out on some cushions. She is dressed in one of Poiret's plain white Directoire gowns. Her interior is a harmony of blue and green. Ornamentation of the gown is at a minimum – blue beads outline the high waistline and are handled with as much geometrical precision as** the interior itself. Poiret's Orientalism is manifested in the close-fitting white turban with a design of small blue dots encircling large blue ones, echoing the colour on the gown. The eyes and mouth of the model are heavily made up. In 1911 Poiret founded Rosine, a house of perfume which also created make-up. He was the first couturier to diversify into perfumes and make-up and to link them to fashion.

a revival of painting, sculpture, architecture, interior decoration and dress. Iribe has stylishly captured the elegance of Poiret's Directoire Revival and the details of the period interior serve to enhance the grace as well as the line of Poiret's creations, very much in the spirit of the Directoire fashion plates of the *Journal des Dames et des Modes*.

While evolving his Directoire style, Poiret did not neglect his other great passion of Orientalia. Orientalism had been a craze since the turn of the century, reaching a peak with the arrival of the Ballets Russes in Paris in 1909. An example of the result of Poiret's eclecticism was illustrated in 1911 by Georges Lepape in *Les choses de Paul Poiret* (fig. 4). Along with André Marty and Charles Martin, Georges Lepape had studied at the Ecole des Beaux-Arts under Fernand-Piestre Cormon, whose former pupils had included Matisse.[6] Again Poiret went back to artistic sources to develop his own particular interpretation of Orientalism. He revived the wearing of turbans which had also been worn very successfully with neo-classical dresses during the Directoire, influenced by the Egyptian campaigns of Napoleon. They abound in the fashion plates of the *Journal des Dames et des Modes* during the period 1797–9 (fig. 5). Besides studying fashion plates, Poiret also discovered that the finest collection of Indian turbans was in the Victoria and Albert Museum in London. Of all the *choses* of Poiret that Lepape drew, the most delightful must surely be those charming turbans.

Building on the work of Iribe, Lepape provides a more complex demonstration of the relationship of fashion with the arts. As if to stress the integration of the dress with the setting, Lepape has entitled his drawing, 'Les coussins', 'The cushions'. The sharp, geometric outlines of the cushions and window, and the stylized floral motif serve perfectly to reinforce the classical

5. **Fashion plate from the** Journal des Dames et des Modes, **25 February 1798. If the** élégantes **of the Directoire aspired to be Grecian goddesses and nymphs with classically inspired gowns, they also sought to enhance their appearance by an aura of mystery from an imagined Orient. They relied principally on exotic turbans, often becomingly decked with an aigrette which served admirably to heighten the statuesque figure. Soldiers from Napoleon's Egyptian campaign brought back Kashmir shawls. They tended to be coloured and contrasted with the white of the gowns, to emphasize the sweep of the drapery and add to the general simplification of shape and movement.**

line of the model's dress and to anchor her in her environment.

As Julian Robinson points out in his book *The Golden Age of Style*, Iribe's treatment of Poiret designs 'marked the beginning of a new era, not only in fashion but in its illustration too, heralding the birth of the style which is known today as *Art Deco* ... He [Lepape] followed Iribe's example'.[7]

It was the *Exposition Internationale des Arts Décoratifs et Industriels Modernes*, held in Paris in 1925, which gave Art Deco its name, for this exhibition was known simply as the *Arts Déco*.[8] This great and vast exhibition had been planned as early as 1915–16; elements of Art Deco were appearing in the work of Paul Poiret and others before the First World War.[9]

Art Déco *then, was an ... eclectic style, drawing on the art of many cultures and countries – and indeed periods ... The 1925* Exposition Internationale des Arts Décoratifs *in Paris drew the different strands together, and helped to bring about some kind of fusion.*[10]

One of these strands, very discernible in the dresses of Poiret, was the neo-classical

6 **'Robes pour l'été, 1920. Il croquis hors-texte de Raoul Dufy'. Featured in the May 1920 issue of the** Gazette du Bon Ton. **The mannequins wear Poiret's summer creations for 1920, made from Dufy designs for the silk firm Bianchini-Férier. The fashionable style of dress was short and loose-fitting with the waistline at its natural level or a tiny bit below, and the skirt either straight and narrowly cut, or very full and bell-shaped. Sometimes the two shapes of skirt were worn together, as seen on the two ladies on the right, who both wear large bows, thus making their skirts the focal point. Headwear also varies – the lady on the far right wears a helmet-shaped hat which comes down to cover her forehead completely; the lady next to her wears a cloche, with a fetching ribbon round the deep crown; the third lady from the left wears a hat with a high crown and upturned brim dashingly tilted to one side; the lady next to her wears a large, wide-brimmed picture hat. An indispensable accessory for the seaside was the parasol.**

our l'été 1920.

line.[11] Indeed, purity of line is one of the hallmarks of the Art Deco style, with the contemporary art movement of Cubism also providing the style with many of its characteristic shapes.[12]

Julian Robinson also made the following perceptive comment on the ways the world of fashion advanced and disseminated the Art Déco style:

> The development of Art Déco was promoted throughout the world during its 'golden years' by a number of high-quality hand-printed books, magazines, albums and periodicals which were published in the twenty-five years between 1908–1932. These publications, with their insight, wit, accuracy, artistry and ingenuity, captured the true spirit of this 'golden age' of style.[13]

The albums of Poiret's designs, produced by Paul Iribe and Georges Lepape, were the first of these publications. It is significant that the important exhibition devoted to Art Déco, Les Années '25', held at the Musée des Arts Décoratifs in Paris in 1966, featured both albums.[14] In 1986, the great retrospective exhibition on Paul Poiret and his sister, Nicole Groult, held at the Musée de la Mode et du Costume in Paris, refers to them on the title page as 'Maîtres de la Mode Art Déco', and features in colour practically all the plates of Iribe and Lepape, including the two examples shown and discussed here.

The enormous success of Poiret's two enterprises sparked off a veritable renaissance in fashion illustration and fashion literature. The year 1912 saw the founding of a new Journal des Dames et des Modes, which, in its title and appearance, followed the tradition of the celebrated periodical of La Mésangère. The Gazette du Bon Ton was also established in 1912. A lavish monthly, the Gazette du Bon Ton united the couturier and the artist in the same way. It featured many of Poiret's designs, drawn by artists such as

Georges Barbier, Georges Lepape, André Marty, Charles Martin, Sim. A. Puget and Raoul Dufy. Relating fashion to the society of the élite, 'when the Gazette du Bon Ton was founded in 1912 it was surely a deliberate attempt to recreate, captions and all, the style of La Mésangère.'[15] The May 1920 issue showed 'Robes pour l'été, 1920. Il croquis hors-texte de Raoul Dufy', an example of the highly successful partnership of Poiret and Dufy (fig. 6). The mannequins wear Poiret dresses made from Dufy's light, airy silks, patterned geometrical motifs derived from Cubism, which he made for the Lyons silk firm, Bianchini-Férier, in 1918–19. These Art Deco designs are a delight – abstract, with bold, fresh, clear colours, underscoring Poiret's summer dresses as eminently suitable for the fashionable to wear by the seaside.

Poiret was continually receptive to new artistic projects and new links with artists. In 1913, he invited the Russian artist Romain de Tirtoff, known in the international fashion and art world as Erté, to become an assistant designer in his fashion house. As well as designing fashionable dress, Erté became involved with Poiret in theatrical costume design. As Erté pointed out in his autobiography, Things I Remember:

> Poiret was the only couturier to have a workshop specialising in theatrical costume design. It was directed by a charming old lady, Madame Régiane, who had formally been 'Première' [head seamstress] with the greatest theatrical costume designer of the day, Landolff.[16]

The culmination of their collaboration was the play entitled Le Minaret, staged in 1913. Many of Erté's fashionable dresses exude a pronounced exoticism which shows direct links to plays with an Oriental flavour. At the same time his drawings demonstrate the advanced work being undertaken in fashion illustration under the aegis of Poiret. Erté considered fashion illustration to be a very important aspect of his art. Poiret called upon him to design models and to make black and white drawings of them for reproduction in fashion magazines.[17] Erté invariably used pen and Indian ink, and also black and white gouache on a spread in tones of grey.

Poiret himself was a very competent painter. After leaving school to work for an umbrella maker, he had relieved the boredom by making, for his own pleasure, sketches of dresses in Indian ink.[18]

Erté had first seen Poiret's dress collections in St Petersburg in 1911, when he made a fashion tour of European capitals, the first ever undertaken by a couturier.[19] Among his other ports of call were Berlin, Munich and Vienna, where Poiret was much inspired by the various schools of decorative arts, such as the Wiener Werkstätte. When he returned to Paris, he launched his interior design school and shop, Martine, named after one of his daughters. A whole range of goods was produced – glass, ceramics, fabrics, wallpaper, curtains, cushions, carpets and furniture. He chose Dufy to help him initiate a whole new direction in textile design. This was the beginning of a long association with Dufy, culminating in the *Exposition Internationale des Arts Décoratifs et Industriels Modernes* in 1925, where Dufy designed dress fabrics and a unique series of wall hangings for Poiret. The organizers of the exhibition were fulsome in acknowledging their debt to Poiret:

> *It is possible to hold this event only because of the impetus that Poiret has given to modern decorative arts by founding the Martine School and shops and encouraging professional interior decorators.*[20]

With the coming of Paul Poiret, fashion, fashion illustration, the theatre, textiles, interior design and even fashion photography underwent an exciting revolution. As the twentieth century has progressed, tributes to the inventiveness of Poiret have been continuous. One cannot help but think that he would have been most pleased with the compliment paid to him by another of the *grands couturiers*, Christian Dior, who, in his autobiography, called Poiret 'this great artist who excelled at creation and decoration'.[21]

1

DIRECTOIRE REVIVAL

The Directoire and First Empire periods apart, European women's costume was traditionally founded on two stiff structures – a bodice which compressed the bust and waist, and a device for extending the skirt of the gown under which it was worn. They were called various names over the centuries: farthingale, *paniers*, corset. Whatever name was used, the natural shape of the body was concealed. When Poiret opened his own fashion house, the era known as *La Belle Epoque* (1900–14) was in full flow and the design style known as Art Nouveau was flourishing. Art Nouveau was characterized by lines that were curving and shapes that were free and flowing. The

leading couturiers, Paquin, Worth and Doucet, under the latter two of whom Poiret served apprenticeships, dressed fashionable society women in an opulent manner which echoed Art Nouveau. Indeed, although as early as 1904 Poiret astonished Jean Worth with a gown based on simple, vertical lines, there exist examples of gowns he created in 1905 in the decorative curves of Art Nouveau.[1]

Literally yards and yards of luxurious materials, in pale, delicate colours, were made up into elaborate, decorated gowns. The sinuous, undulating lines of the gowns were achieved by using a new type of corset, invented in 1902, called the *Gache Sarraute*.[2] It produced an S-curved line and hence the silhouette became known as the S-bend. The S-bend figure had a large bosom and hips and a minute waist, as the corset threw the bust forward and the hips back. The gown illustrated here, designed by Doucet, was typical: a high neck, with a frilly bodice, elbow-length sleeves, very full undersleeves gathered into tight cuffs at the wrists. The skirt is cut straight at the front, the fullness at the back extending into a long train. Lace was one of the most popular fabrics for gowns and Doucet chose a frothy Venetian lace (fig. 7). Poiret came to call women who dressed in this way 'decorated bundles'.[3]

Poiret's first great 'revolution', as he called it, was to 'wage war' on the *Gache Sarraute*. This was well underway by 1906:

> *The last representative of this abominable apparatus was called the* Gache Sarraute. *It divided the wearer into two distinct masses: on one side there was the bust and bosom, on the other, the whole behindward aspect, so that the lady looked as if she were hauling a trailer. It was almost a return to the bustle. Like all great revolutions, that one had been made in the name of Liberty – to give free play to the abdomen: it was equally in the name of Liberty that I proclaimed the fall of the corset and the adoption of the brassière which, since then, has won the day.*[4]

Having jettisoned these constricting foundations, Poiret went on to establish his classical line of dress. In his autobiography he related how his father had been a cloth merchant and how he had been sent by him to work for an umbrella maker. Poiret hated the work but was often able to escape to the Louvre to study paintings and ancient sculpture.[5]

> *While studying sculptures of ancient times, I learned to use one point of support – the shoulders, where before me it had been the waist. All my gowns flowed from that point of support at the extremity of the shoulders and were never fastened at the waist. This new basic principle caused fashion to evolve toward classical antiquity ... Fabrics flowed from this ideal point like water from a fountain and draped the body in a way that was entirely natural.*[6]

As discussed earlier, this style of dress was labelled Directoire, after the fashions of the period 1795–9. A pronounced sculptural quality was what the dresses of the Directoire had in common. They were designed in the manner of classical Greek drapery, to reveal the natural shape and contours of the body. With their high waistlines and long, straight lines, the effect was clearly to elongate the body and make it more statuesque.

While muslin, because of its fluid and transparent qualities, was the main material used to obtain the classical line, the Directoire dresses that survive in the Musée de la Mode et du Costume and the Musée des Arts de la Mode in Paris, as well as the fashion plates in La Mésangère's *Journal des Dames et des Modes*, show that other materials, such as light silks, satins and tulle were also very popular and could also achieve the same intended effect.

Poiret certainly must have studied the Directoire fashion plates of the *Journal des Dames et des Modes*. He had served his main apprenticeship in the couture house of the exalted Jacques Doucet, whose whole setting, recalled Poiret, 'was composed of engravings and pictures of the eighteenth century, and of rare and ancient furniture'.[7] The Bibliothèque Doucet, the art library of the University of Paris, houses the books and art collections of its namesake. It is significant that the Bibliothèque Doucet is the only public library in France with a complete set of the *Journal des Dames et des Modes* for the Directoire period. The Russian artist Erté noted in his autobiography that when he came to work for Poiret, 'all the salons in his fashion house were decorated in Directoire style'.[8]

Poiret's Directoire Revival fashions were being purchased by 1907, for Lady Diana Cooper recalled in her memoirs, *The Rainbow Comes and Goes*, that there came from Paris, via Princess Murat, 'the glad tidings of the rising star Poiret, an eccentricity, a new word, and a new mania'.[9]

> *Greek – everything must be Greek. I*

must draw a bow and have a crescent in my hair, draperies, sandalled or bare feet (dragging at the second toe to make it longer than the big one), peplums, archaic smiles, shining white limbs of the godlike youths in the river, Pan pipes, Butcher and Lang's Homer readings, and human statues photographed on pedestals. There is a bust that Mackennal made of me with Grecian curls and a crescent and the rest of it.

Fashion had come round to us. Gone were the buttoned boots, the curves, the boned collars, the straight-fronted stays, the hennaed hair and hair-nets.[10]

Poiret's Directoire silhouette must have been considered quite revolutionary, as Madame Paquin, one of the leading fashion designers, was still featuring the S-bend as late as 1911.[11] Poiret was asked to contribute an article to the high-brow literary magazine *La Grande Revue* in May 1909, elucidating his aesthetic principles on women's dress, 'an extraordinary honour for a dress designer to be included in an organ of this quality'.[12] One of his themes was a call for a return to the Directoire concept of naturalness and simplicity. It was illustrated by another of the fine artists of the time, who also became a friend of Poiret, Jean-Louis Boussingault. Boussingault was an exceptionally good painter who won acclaim at the Salon des Indépendants.[13] Again, he was one of those subtle draughtsman, who, with very few lines, could effectively convey Poiret's conception of the Directoire style. He placed a svelte Poiretesque figure against a 'decorated bundle' (fig. 8). The provenance for this type of illustration can be traced back to the Directoire when the outstanding artist Alexis Chataignier engraved prints contrasting a Directoire *élégante* with a fashionable lady of the *ancien régime* encased in her *paniers*,

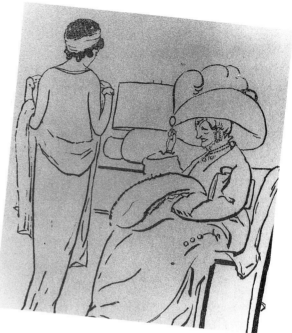

8 **Drawing by Jean-Louis Boussingault to accompany Poiret's fashion article in** La Grande Revue, **May 1909. Poiret also promoted the Directoire Revival by writing about it. The well-upholstered matron with her S-shaped figure closely examines the fashionable young lady in her Directoire Revival creation by Poiret. Boussingault is showing the movement from the curving Art Nouveau style of the elderly lady to Poiret's slim, vertical line under neo-classical inspiration which was by now firmly established.**

adding captions reflecting what the two ladies thought on seeing each other: 'How old fashioned! What a novelty!'

Poiret could also shock, as in Directoire times, by having a group of his models besport themselves at the Longchamps races:

The girls wore identical Hellenic gowns with the sides slit from the knees down to disclose calves and ankles in coloured stockings ... From all sides screams of fright and outrage greeted them ... 'I shall have the charity to refrain from mentioning the couturier who is guilty of this outrage' ... 'To think of it! Under those straight gowns we could sense their bodies.'[14]

During the Directoire, when ladies dared to parade down the Champs Elysées in gauze sheath dresses, the crowd gave proof of its moral fibre by trying to lynch them. Another lady revealed so many of her charms among the gardens at Tivoli that she was forced by an indignant crowd to take refuge in the orangerie. An avid female correspondent of La Mésangère pointed out in the *Journal des Dames et des Modes* that she envied the Greeks their lack of inhibitions about nudity and threatened to foresake the gardens of Tivoli altogether unless she were allowed to show more of herself there. However, so fastidious were the bulk of the Directoire *élégantes*, if only because of popular intolerance, that they even took care, according to La Mésangère, to cover their arms and shoulders with a shawl. His reports suggest that the laws of decency were being scrupulously observed by the *élégantes*.[15] The same could be said of Poiret's creations. His gowns, while engaging, were very chaste in appearance.

The most exquisite of the Directoire *élégantes*, and noted patron of neo-classical taste, in particular of sculpture, was Joséphine de Beauharnais, the future empress and consort of Napoleon.[16] Mme Deslandres, in her interesting article on Josephine, noted that during the Directoire:

> ... *she delighted to wear those close-fitting dresses, of white embroidered muslin, of lawn with gold and silver threads, of light silk woven with scattered sprigs, which are illustrated in the engravings of the* Journal des Dames et des Modes ... *Josephine ran into debt so that she could appear for a single evening wearing a sheath gown to which real rose-petals had been stuck.*[17]

Another form of the classically inspired Directoire style which she particularly favoured was the chemise or sheath gown worn with a knee-length tunic, which also featured in the *Journal des Dames et des Modes*. She continued to wear this style throughout the Consulate because she liked it so much.

Josephine epitomized all the grace and elegance of the Directoire. So it is fitting that Poiret should have named one of his most purist Directoire creations the 'tunique Joséphine' (fig. 9). It appeared in Paul Iribe's *Les robes de Paul Poiret*. The neo-classical costume is set off against a Directoire commode and is emphasized by the piece of classical statuary and the portrait of Lady Hamilton by George Romney. The ensemble consisted of a long, straight dress with short sleeves made in white satin. Over the dress is a black tulle tunic with gold braid round the neck, waist and sleeves, and a border of gold braid spirals at the hem. The only other decoration is a rose, Poiret's logo, found on his stationery and dress labels. It is symbolic that roses were Josephine's favourite flowers and were the floral motif most often seen on her dresses.[18] The 'tunique Joséphine' is still beautifully intact today.[19]

The inclusion of the statue and portrait of Lady Hamilton demonstrate that Poiret had researched the Directoire well, for the hairstyle was considered an important adjunct to the dress. For late-eighteenth-century fashionable society Lady Hamilton was the modeller of Grecian dress, who brought the antique to life. Dressed in her neo-classical costume, and wearing her hair with stylized curls and encircled with a Grecian-style fillet, she gave performances of classical dances before mesmerized

9 'La tunique Joséphine' by Paul Poiret. From Les robes de Paul Poiret racontées par Paul Iribe, 1908. The exquisite 'Joséphine' model consists of a long, high-waisted dress in white satin with a black tulle tunic edged with gold braid. The Directoire commode, statue and portrait of Lady Hamilton enhance Poiret's interpretation of the neo-classical style.

audiences at the British Embassy in Naples. These were subsequently widely imitated in France. Poiret gave his model the same hairstyle and fillet seen in the portrait of Lady Hamilton.

The theme of gown and tunic was a favourite of Poiret's and he was continually experimenting with variations on it. One outstanding example was his 'Robe Strozzi' which appeared in the magazine *Art et Décoration* in April 1911 (fig. 10). The gown was overlaid with two tunics differing in length and colours. The colours of the ensemble shade from violet to green and the hems of the tunics are edged with brilliants. A happy eclecticism is found here as in the Directoire. The neo-classical and the Oriental co-existed perfectly, the turban with an aigrette enhancing the elongation of the figure. The model's backdrop was a salon in Poiret's fashion house where one can see to advantage one of the superb Directoire interiors recalled by Erté. The interior and the costume complement and harmonize admirably, well served by the technique of soft-focus photography worked out by Poiret and the American photographer and painter Edward Steichen.[20] The combination of gown and tunic was a style Poiret made his own. Assessing Poiret in her book, *Always in Vogue*, Edith Woolman Chase (who had been editor of the American, British and French editions of *Vogue*) wrote that 'the flaring yet slim tunic and modern silhouette were to a great extent his

10 *'Robe Strozzi' by Paul Poiret, 1911. This shows two tunics, one on top of the other. The colours of the ensemble shade harmoniously from the green of the sheath gown to the violet of the bodice of the outer tunic. The turban is encircled by a piece of lamé and held in place by a buckle and surmounted by an aigrette. A whole series of Poiret designs, including this one, appeared in the April 1911 issue of* Art et Décoration, *all photographed by Edward Steichen. Poiret supervised the backgrounds, the poses of the models and the lighting.*

innovation'.[21]

It is a mark of Poiret's genius that out of such simplicity he charmed so many delightful variations. The basic theme was swiftly copied by other couture houses. An example of his influence was the 'Rose Dress' or toilette for a garden party designed by his former mentor, Jacques Doucet, which appeared in the *Gazette du Bon Ton* in May 1913 (see plate 6). Its most striking detail is the two-tiered tunic motif which creates a floating effect due to the soft, fluid pleats. Other engaging ideas are the ingenious use of scarves, which enjoyed a great vogue during the Directoire and Empire periods. The model's bodice features a muslin fichu, around the top of which is tied a small rose bow-tie. Attractive, too, is the 'Empire scarf' tied around the waist and draped over the arm.

The same year that Doucet's dress appeared in the *Gazette du Bon Ton*, the *Journal des Dames et des Modes* showed an evening dress in tulle and satin, drawn by George Barbier. It consists of a long, narrow skirt and an off-the-shoulder tunic which has beautifully fluted pleats (fig. 11). The streamlined elegance of the dress is reinforced by the sharp geometric outlines of the blue velvet sash weighted with pearls. The mannequin is silhouetted against an interior remarkably similar to that of the Poiret model wearing the 'Robe Strozzi'. It will be noticed that the skirt is so narrow that it has a slight slit up the front.

In his autobiography Poiret pronounced that while he 'freed the bust' he 'shackled the legs'.[22] For one of his collections in 1910 he took his slim, straight, Directoire style to its most incongruous extent – the hobble skirt (fig. 12). The skirt of the high-waisted gowns became so narrow that it was almost impossible to walk. To prevent the material of her dress from splitting the fashionable lady had to have the bottom held in by straps or tapes so that she could

11 Gala evening gown in tulle and satin, with a velvet sash weighted with pearls. A fashion plate from the Journal des Dames et des Modes, *1913. Georges Barbier, a prolific painter, theatre designer and fashion illustrator shows here his mastery of precise, geometrical design allied to a vivid palette suggesting the influence of* Les choses de Paul Poiret vues par Georges Lepape.

3

Atelier Bachwitz

12 **Fashion plate from** Chic Parisien, **1911. The Directoire Revival suit shows the neat, trim, tailored look of 1911. The long skirt is so narrow that it hindered walking and was aptly called the hobble skirt or** la jupe entravée **by the French. The original** élégante **of the Directoire period adopted masculine features in her attire, including a cutaway jacket with large, plain cloth buttons and wide lapels, derived from the masculine riding coat, a lacy** fichu-cravate **and large square-cut silver shoe buckles, all worn here by her twentieth-century counterpart. The high waist of the jacket is defined by a belt. The headwear of the original** élégantes **assumed such a bewildering variety of forms that some of them could not have walked down the streets of Athens at any date in antiquity without causing consternation. Headwear during the Directoire Revival also reflected a variety of styles, including large, wide-brimmed picture hats, often bedecked with ribbons, bows, flowers and feathers. They were named after Gainsborough's portrait of the Duchess of Devonshire who had been a popular figure in late eighteenth-century fashionable society in England and in France.**

13 **Three draped gowns by Paul Poiret. From** Les robes de Paul Poiret racontées par Paul Iribe, **1908. The model on the left wears a plain white gown and a bright yellow sleeveless tunic fastened with long cords bearing tassels and jewels. The model in the centre wears a blue-green gown with a design echoing the trees seen through the window behind. The model on the right wears under her gown a skirt so finely pleated that it evokes certain celebrated creations of Fortuny. Poiret borrowed the idea of using decorative buttons from the** incroyables, **the young fops of the Directoire period. Iribe himself designed similar** toilettes **in 1912 for the actresses to wear in** Rue de la Paix, **an example of fashion influencing the theatre.**

take only small, mincing steps. Although there were outcries from various quarters, including campaigns to wage war on it, the hobble skirt persisted as a fashion well after the First World War and there was 'hobbling' not only in Paris but in other European capitals and in America.[23]

Throughout his Hellenic phase, Poiret rejected surface decoration of the dress itself. As in the Directoire, he preferred to add some striking trimming or accessory which animated but never obtruded on the neo-classical line. Poiret used large, decorative buttons with panache. Their source can be traced back to the *incroyables*, the young fops of the Directoire.[24] In another of Iribe's illustrations in *Les robes de Paul Poiret* of 1908, featuring a group of three Directoire gowns, one in particular captures our attention (fig. 13). The model on the right wears a long-sleeved gown made in mauve satin gauze and purple crêpe de Chine, which forms an attractive striped pattern. Her straight skirt opens out on the left to reveal a very finely pleated mauve chiffon

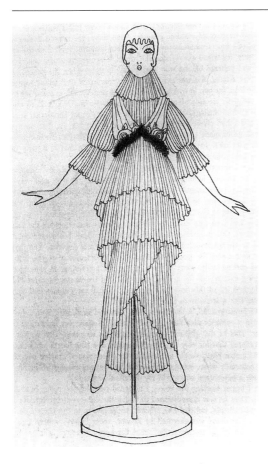

**14 Dress design for Paul Poiret by Erté, 1913.
Erté has transferred a theatrical costume design
to fashionable dress. It exemplifies all the fluidity,
elegance, glamour and exoticism that appealed
to Poiret.**

underskirt, and is held in place at the top by a row of five large buttons in gold, red and green braid. The high waistline is accentuated by a drawstring made of gold braid with gold tassels. In 1912 Poiret took the idea further with his 'Fleurie' gown, where the high waistline is emphasized by two huge bronze buttons. This dress is still in a pristine state today.[25]

A salient example of Poiret's use of accessories and trimmings together is 'The Yellow Gown' from Lepape's album of 1911. The high waist is held in place by a belt with tassels. Tassels were a favourite accessory with Poiret 'which took inspiration from the Doric *peplos*.[26] The red of the belt and tassels heightens the brilliance of the yellow of the gown and this effect is further intensified by the use of dark fur as a trimming on the sleeves and hem. Fur was another Oriental borrowing but it is handled with as much restraint and precision as the classical-style belt and tassels.

By 1913 the theatre was influencing the fashions of the Directoire Revival. Erté was now flourishing in Poiret's fashion house and much involved in the theatrical workshop located there. Both were passionately interested in the theatre and, according to Erté, they often went to see plays together:

*He often invited me to accompany him
to the theatre, and in this way I saw
many splendid performances. I
remember best the gala opening of the
new Théâtre des Champs-Elysées. I
have never seen a more brilliant
audience: the women blazed with
jewels. That year they were wearing
tulle scarfs about their bare shoulders,
for dresses were very* décolleté. *They
seemed to rise, nude, out of fluffy
clouds. Every woman wore a head-
dress: dazzling tiaras, embroidered
bandeaux, or turbans with aigrettes
and birds-of-paradise plumes.*[27]

The theatre was one of the most popular

venues for the fashionable to show off
their finery, just like the original *élégantes*
of the Directoire. And just like their
historical counterparts, they clamoured for
the enchanting creations they saw on the
stage, many of which were adapted for
fashionable day and evening wear and for
fancy dress parties and balls.

Poiret and Erté were fortunate in being
asked to collaborate on the costume
designs for many plays. Erté recorded that
fashion for 1913 was influenced by the
costumes they created for one play, *Le
Minaret*. As has been pointed out, the neo-
classical fashions of the Directoire period
were infused with a mysterious charm
from the East through the wearing of
Kashmir shawls, turbans and aigrettes and
the use of fur as a trimming. Poiret, as has
been seen, continued in this tradition. His
specific affiliation with the theatre is
admirably depicted by Erté (fig. 14). The
sheer muslin dress, with its two tiers
creating a tunic effect, has an exotic
accessory attached to the bodice that is
taken directly from a costume design for
Le Minaret (fig. 29). This is made of silk
with large stylized floral embroidery and
fur trim. It has the effect of pulling in the
high waist and describing the graceful
curves of the bust. The inspiration for this
accessory may in some measure have come
from the Directoire. Many of the fashion
plates in La Mésangère's *Journal des
Dames et des Modes* show details on the
bodices of dresses that were derived from
theatrical designs (fig. 15). Fichus, spencers,
and shawls were also used to achieve the
same effect (fig. 5). La Mésangère declared
that far from constraining the outline of
the bust, the natural contours of the
breasts were emphasized.[28] The *élégantes*
invariably wore turbans and aigrettes with
these costumes to obtain a coherent
ensemble.

Poiret also designed especially for some
of the great actresses of the period. His
'Salomé' gown was adapted from one of his

15   *Fashion plate from the* Journal des Dames et
des Modes *for 11 February 1798. Challenges to
dress of the Directoire age included various
accessories for the bodice which were derived
mainly from the theatre. Neo-classical costume
admirably showed its powers of absorption. It is a
tribute to the strength of Poiret's Directoire style
that his ensembles with theatrical overtones could
also enhance the dress. The theatre, including
the ballet and opera, of both periods fascinated
the fashionable lady. The theatre filled the role of
unofficial fashion parade where the costumes of
the actresses, dancers and singers often set the
fashion for the audience.*

creations for Ida Rubinstein. Its success as a fashion is attested by its appearance in the *Gazette du Bon Ton* in March 1914, drawn by Sim. A. Puget (fig. 16). An evening gown made of tulle, it is edged with jet beads, a favourite Oriental motif. A most striking feature is the bodice with its exquisite embroidery forming a group of swirling stylized floral patterns that appear again on the skirt and stockings. It is a design repeatedly seen on Poiret costumes and interior décor (fig. 30). The same motif can be found on many of the costumes of the Ballets Russes.[29] The model's jewellery also derives from the Orient. It consists of long jet earrings and strands of pearls, the preferred jewellery of the Directoire *élégantes*, as they not only provided colour contrast but were elongated, thus complementing the costume.

Poiret's Directoire Revival, whether in its purist form or combined with Oriental details, was truly revolutionary. The original concept of over a hundred years before, on which it was based, the natural shape of the figure, has been fundamental to fashion ever since.

16 *'Salomé' by Paul Poiret. Drawn by Sim. A. Puget, 1914. An evening gown of pleated black tulle on a white ground. The skirts are tiered, falling from a high, well-defined waistline edged with large pearls. This evening gown was adapted from one of Poiret's creations for the actress Ida Rubinstein.*

2
ORIENTALISM

French society had a long tradition of being fascinated with the Orient. In the seventeenth century the East India Company brought lacquer goods and porcelains back to Paris. *Chinoiserie*, the fanciful imitation of Chinese art by the West, was an important decorative style in the eighteenth century. Chinese influence manifested itself in interior design, furniture, porcelain and textiles. Popular dress fabrics featured designs of Chinese landscapes containing pagodas, mandarins and parasols. During the Directoire and Empire periods, the two great themes in dress were neo-classicism and Orientalism, which, as has been pointed out, perfectly complemented one another.

So it is not surprising that at the beginning of the twentieth century Orientalism would again become a craze, and that Parisian theatregoers would respond enthusiastically to the arrival of the Ballets Russes in 1909. The sets and costume designs by the Russian painter Léon Bakst for ballets such as *Schéhérazade* in 1910 and *Dioné* in 1912, with their exotic patterns, brilliant colours and lush fabrics, dazzled the audiences and

inspired artists, interior decorators and couturiers (fig. 17). For Bakst, the Ballets Russes and Orientalism, especially Poiret's interpretation of it, provided the Art Deco style with more ingredients – colour and surface decoration.[1] Art Deco replaced the pastel shades of Art Nouveau with a veritable explosion of colour – orange, green, red and purple. Fabrics made in these colours were enriched with much surface decoration, such as silver and gold, embroidery, beading and fur.

Poiret claimed that the Ballets Russes and Léon Bakst had not played any really significant role in his own interpretation of Orientalism:

Like many French artists, I was struck by the Russian Ballet, and I should not be surprised if it had a certain influence on me. But it must be clearly stated that I already existed, and that my reputation was made, long before that of M. Bakst.[2]

Indeed, Poiret was right. His cloak, based on the kimono, which he called 'Confucius' (see page 34), appeared well before the arrival of the Ballets Russes and Bakst, and he had been selling his turbans since 1906.[3] As early as 1907 some of his

31

17 'Dioné-dessin de Bakst réalisé par Paquin', 1912. This shows Orientalism combined with Directoire Revival. In 1913, the Journal des Dames et des Modes **published this costume design by Léon Bakst for the Ballets Russes production of** Dioné. **The lavish surface decoration and the bold yellow and orange colouring of the costume reflected the taste for Orientalism, while the fashionable, neo-classical line and shape persisted.**

Oriental fashions had already reached England. Lady Diana Cooper recalled in her memoirs a stunning creation that Princess Murat wore and her own great success in copying it:

> *It was a chiffon shirt worn in the evening over a skirt. It was cut like an Eastern djibbah and edged at the hem and Eastern neckline with braid. I elaborated the design, even to putting fur instead of braid, and made them by the dozen for friends and friends' friends. They cost me about fifteen shillings and I charged two guineas. I made over a hundred pounds, all of which I spent on books –* éditions de luxe *and first editions, the Edinburgh Stevenson, Meredith and Wilde, Conrad and Maupassant. I owed a lot to Poiret and made him ridiculous no doubt, by my base imitations.*[4]

As has already been noted, Poiret had often given his Directoire Revival an Oriental twist. If his autobiography is read carefully, it is clear that the germ of his intense interest in the Orient was laid in his extreme youth when he was made by his father to undertake tedious work for an umbrella maker.

> *When I was back at home in the evening I withdrew into my room and imagined sumptuous toilettes, faery panoplies. My sister had presented me with a wooden mannequin forty centimetres high, and on this little model I pinned my silks and muslins. What delightful evenings I owed to this doll, whom I made successively a piquante Parisienne and an Eastern Queen.*
>
> *And then I designed fantastical ensembles. My sketches were summaries, they were notations in Indian ink, and I remember that the idea was always clearly indicated, and that there was always some inventive detail, some interesting special point.*[5]

As early as 1898–9, when he was serving

his apprenticeship at Chez Doucet, his most successful creation was a cloak.

> *My first model was a little cloak in red cloth, with bands of cloth pinked around the neck. There was a lapel of grey crêpe de Chine with which it was lined, and it buttoned up one side with six enamel buttons. Five hundred copies were sold. Fair clients wanted it in every colour. Henceforth my position was assured.*[6]

One day the celebrated actress Réjane came to see Doucet about costuming her for the play *Zaza*. Doucet, knowing of Poiret's love of the theatre, immediately let him into their confidence, telling him about the play and suggesting he design a cloak especially for Réjane to wear in the final act. In his autobiography Poiret recalled how overwhelmed he was by such an honour. For the dress historian, however, it is his original sense of design at such an early stage in his career, as well as his superb handling of materials and striking use of colours, that are truly overwhelming.

> *From that moment I could not sleep, none of my ideas seemed to me beautiful enough or in any way worthy of Réjane. Finally I did make a cloak. It was of black tulle, veiling a black taffeta that had been painted by Billoty [a fan-painter then famous] with immense white and mauve irises. An enormous ribbon of mauve satin and another of violet satin running across the tulle joined the shoulders and closed the cloak in front with a cunning knot. All the sadness of a romantic dénouement, all the bitterness of a fourth act, were in this so-expressive cloak, and when they saw it appear, the audience foresaw the end of the play ... Thenceforth, I was established, Chez Doucet and in Paris. I had stormed the ramparts on the shoulders of Réjane.*[7]

The great Doucet not only recognized his prodigious talent but accepted and encouraged it. Theirs was an intelligent collaboration, confirmed by the approval of the clientele of La Maison Doucet.

When Poiret moved on, however, in 1901, to join La Maison Worth, the most prestigious fashion house of all, his creativity did not meet with the same enthusiasm. His kimono, a cloak of Oriental inspiration, designed for the Russian Princess Bariatinsky, was considered just a little too *outré* for the princess, as Poiret recalled in 1930:

> *M. Worth most obsequiously made her sit down, while the mannequins appeared with speed, and I had the honour of showing the Princess a cloak I had just finished, and which was then a novelty. Today it would seem banal, almost outmoded, but then nothing like it had been seen. It was a great square kimono in black cloth, bordered with black satin cut obliquely; the sleeves were wide right to the bottom, and were finished with embroidered cuffs like the sleeves of Chinese mantles. Did the Princess have some vision of China, which for Russia bore a hostile face? Did she see Port Arthur, or something other? I know not, but she cried out: 'Ah! What a horror; with us, when there are low fellows who run after our sledges and among us, we have their heads cut off, and we put them in sacks just like that ...'*[8]

Poiret took the hint and, with the loan of his mother's savings, established his own fashion house in vacant premises at 5 rue Auber at the corner of the rue Scribe. It was opened formally on 1 September 1903. One of his first clients was Réjane. With her patronage his career was well and truly launched. The incident at La Maison Worth was not forgotten, however, and provided the beginning of a whole host of original creations in the Oriental mode.

One day Réjane came in ... The

memory of Princess Bariatinsky haunted me, and the cloak she had reproved seemed to me more and more beautiful. It was to become the type of a whole series of creations. And might one not still say, today [1930], that there is something of this model in the cloaks that are made everywhere? In any case, for years, it dominated and inspired the mode. I called it 'Confucius'. Every woman bought at least one. It was the beginning of the Oriental influence in fashion, of which I had made myself the apostle.[9]

The simple lines and brilliant colours of Poiret's Oriental style are beautifully evoked in *Les robes de Paul Poiret recontées par Paul Iribe*, published in 1908, a year before the arrival of the Ballets Russes. A most striking example is the drawing entitled 'Trois manteaux', plate 9 of the album. The *manteau* in the centre is derived from the 'Confucius' cloak (see plate 2). This was an exotic Hispahan coat made in sumptuous green cotton velvet, embroidered with Persian palms sharply outlined in bold yellow and white. Two other coats of differing lengths frame the Hispahan coat. They are in shades of yellow and mustard and trimmed with fur. The contrasting front and back views show off the vertical lines of the garments to advantage. Further contrasts of vivid colours are provided by the three dresses just visible beneath the coats, showing off blocks of royal blue, red and white. A riot of colour is also echoed in the hairstyle and the headbands and headscarf – a veritable palette of sensuous red, black, blue, green, orange and pink.

This plate, with its format of clear, flat areas of colour and assymetrical arrangement of the models, shows the influence of Japanese prints which had been such a rich source for artists in the nineteenth century, such as Manet, Gauguin and Van Gogh. In order to attain colours of such jewel-like brilliance, a special technique called the *pochoir* process was used by Iribe. *Pochoir*, which means stencil, was a method whereby a monochrome print was hand-coloured using a series of bronze or zinc stencils. The *pochoir* process, being manual rather than mechanical, was very slow and painstaking, building up each area of colour and reproducing all the varying shades of the original. Poiret and publishers like Lucien Vogel of the *Gazette du Bon Ton* aimed for a very high quality of reproduction, trying to capture an image as close as possible to the original.

In his autobiography Poiret laid stress on the importance of colour and, more particularly, on his own new colour scheme:

... on the pretext that it was 'distinguished', all vitality had been suppressed. Nuances of nymphs' thighs, lilacs, swooning mauves, tender blue hortensias, nile greens, maizes, straws, all that was soft, washed-out, insipid was held in honour. I threw into this sheepcote a few rough wolves; reds, greens, violets, royal blues, that made all the rest sing aloud. I had to wake up the good people of Lyons, whose stomach is a bit heavy, and put a little gaiety, a little freshness, into their colour schemes. There were orange and lemon crêpes de Chine which they would not have dared to imagine. On the other hand, the morbid mauves were hunted out of existence: there appeared a new dawn – the gamut of pastel shades. I carried with me the colourists when I took each tone at its most vivid, and I restored to health all the exhausted nuances. I am truly forced to accord myself the merit of all this.[10]

Poiret's colour sense was very akin to the palette of the Fauve painters. At the Salon d'Automne of 1905, held in Paris, the works of a number of painters, many of them friends of Poiret, were hung together

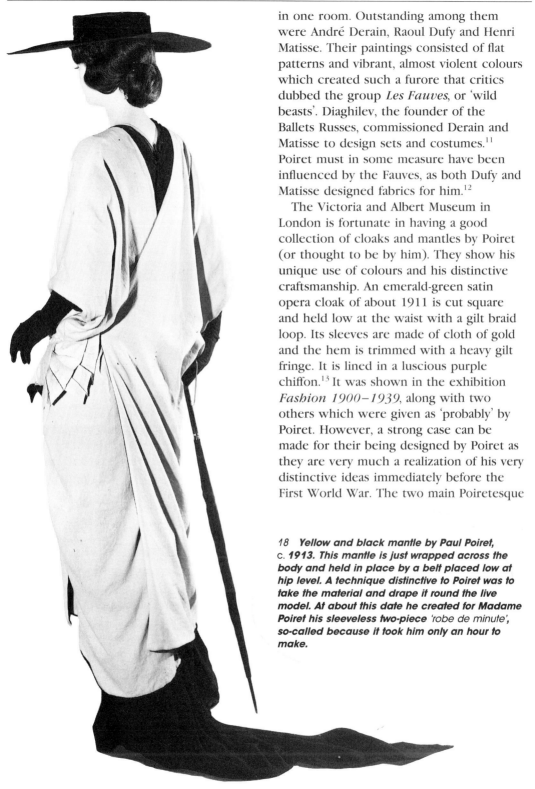

in one room. Outstanding among them were André Derain, Raoul Dufy and Henri Matisse. Their paintings consisted of flat patterns and vibrant, almost violent colours which created such a furore that critics dubbed the group *Les Fauves*, or 'wild beasts'. Diaghilev, the founder of the Ballets Russes, commissioned Derain and Matisse to design sets and costumes.[11] Poiret must in some measure have been influenced by the Fauves, as both Dufy and Matisse designed fabrics for him.[12]

The Victoria and Albert Museum in London is fortunate in having a good collection of cloaks and mantles by Poiret (or thought to be by him). They show his unique use of colours and his distinctive craftsmanship. An emerald-green satin opera cloak of about 1911 is cut square and held low at the waist with a gilt braid loop. Its sleeves are made of cloth of gold and the hem is trimmed with a heavy gilt fringe. It is lined in a luscious purple chiffon.[13] It was shown in the exhibition *Fashion 1900–1939*, along with two others which were given as 'probably' by Poiret. However, a strong case can be made for their being designed by Poiret as they are very much a realization of his very distinctive ideas immediately before the First World War. The two main Poiretesque

18 Yellow and black mantle by Paul Poiret, c. 1913. This mantle is just wrapped across the body and held in place by a belt placed low at hip level. A technique distinctive to Poiret was to take the material and drape it round the live model. At about this date he created for Madame Poiret his sleeveless two-piece 'robe de minute', so-called because it took him only an hour to make.

LE MANTEAU DE POURPRE

Manteau du soir de Paul Poiret

elements, a combination of sensuous colours and a fluidity of line, are prominently displayed. A knee-length mantle of about 1913, in orange and fuchsia velvet, is embroidered with a curving pattern in gold thread and lined with golden yellow.[14] Another mantle, also dated about 1913, is in contrasting colours of yellow and black (fig. 18). It is made of separate panels of yellow wool lined in black silk, wrapped around the figure and held in place by a belt with a bow as a trimming, that is fastened very low.[15] This mantle serves to illustrate well the dressmaker as artist, because its total effect as an ensemble comes from both the colours and the graceful arrangement of folds of material around the body, rather than from the cut of the mantle itself. It was Dior who recalled that Poiret:

> ... *used to take the material in his hands, drape it softly around the figure of his mannequin, without worrying too much how it fell. He relied on startling colours,*
> *then a snip here and there, a few pins ...*[16]

Over the months and years the *Gazette du Bon Ton* featured a pleiad of lavish plates depicting Poiret's coats, capes, cloaks and mantles. In the February 1914 issue Georges Lepape drew a Poiret coat which showed what elaborate effects could be achieved by the use of velvet and fur (fig. 19). 'Le Manteau de Pourpre' was one of Poiret's most flamboyant creations. The coat of purple velvet cascades from an enormous piece of ermine which extends into very long, full sleeves. In spite of its daring, even amusing quality, Poiret has nevertheless imbued the coat with one of his major Oriental design elements, the silhouette and line of the kimono. This is

20 'Danaé'. Evening cape by Paul Poiret. Drawn by Charles Martin, 1914. Poiret's unique evocation of fantasy. His capes were often made of so much material that they entirely encircled their wearer from neck to feet and even extended beyond, as this model demonstrates. Printing on velvet, a material rich in itself, was something new at the time. Its provenance was the examples produced by Dufy when he was working with Poiret and the Martines at the Petite Usine in 1911.

19 'Le Manteau de Pourpre'. Evening coat by Paul Poiret. Drawn by Georges Lepape, 1914. This is one of Poiret's most spectacular Oriental creations. A very fantastic and daring way of using fur as a decorative accessory.

21 *'Have I come too early?' Theatre coat by Paul Poiret. Drawn by Georges Lepape, 1912. Made in yellow silk with a skunk fur collar. The clasp and the arm slits are embroidered in shimmering blue-green silk threads. It is lined in blue-green satin.*

reflected in the way the velvet is draped in an unstructured manner round the body from behind. Even the fur retains the spirit of the kimono by the fact that the sleeves are not separate, tubular entities, but rather extensions of the body of the ermine itself.

The May 1914 issue of the *Gazette* showed Charles Martin's dramatic drawing entitled 'Danaé', depicting a cape as a swirling mass of red velvet trimmed with gold and offset by a huge black velvet collar (fig. 20). It is lined in black velvet printed with the little dots and small, spotted circles seen on so many of the costumes of the Ballets Russes.[17]

The *Gazette du Bon Ton* invariably subtitled these garments 'Manteau du soir de Paul Poiret', 'Cape du soir de Paul Poiret', etc. They were meant to be worn in the evening and their sheer dash brought in a whole new conception of evening wear. This was underscored in the *Gazette* which often showed these garments being worn in enchanting nocturnal settings. The November 1912 issue, for example, showed a model holding a programme to her face and coquettishly inquiring 'Serais-je en avance?' ('Have I come too early?') (fig. 21). Her coat was designed specially to be worn for an evening out at the theatre. The drawing by Georges Lepape captures Poiret's love of supple materials and colour contrasts. The theatre coat is made of yellow silk and decorated with delicate embroidery in shimmering blue-green silk threads. The revers, turned back and held in place by a gold link chain, reveal a blue-green satin lining. Poiret, who both fostered the use of fur and exploited fur in fashion to the full during his Oriental phase, chose here to

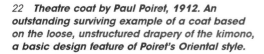

22 Theatre coat by Paul Poiret, 1912. An outstanding surviving example of a coat based on the loose, unstructured drapery of the kimono, a basic design feature of Poiret's Oriental style.

23 *'Le Lys Rouge – Robe du soir de Paul Poiret'.*
Drawn by Sim. A. Puget, 1914. An evening gown
consisting of a gold tunic and a black and green
embroidered skirt. La Maison Poiret was
renowned for its excellence of embroidery allied
to distinctive design.

make the huge collar of skunk fur.

A very similar theatre coat, designed by Poiret in 1912, is now in the Costume Institute of the Metropolitan Museum in New York (fig. 22). It is made of yellow and pale blue charmeuse and trimmed with black velvet and silver lace. It is interesting to see the two theatre coats side by side. The fashion plate in the *Gazette du Bon Ton* is like a vignette evoking the languid world of the wealthy élite at one of their favourite venues, the theatre. The subject is an elegant woman wearing one of Poiret's most beautiful coats in the Oriental mode – it is a symphony of line and colour. The actual specimen demonstrates not only this but also, as Jean Druesedow points out in her stimulating article in the *Metropolitan Museum of Art Bulletin*, the 'texture of the fabrication'.[18]

The costumes worn beneath these evening wraps were equally luxurious and sensuous. 'Le Lys Rouge – Robe du soir de Paul Poiret' appeared in the April 1914 issue of the *Gazette du Bon Ton*, drawn by Sim. A. Puget. (fig. 23) This ensemble consists of a gold tunic with a low waist, emphasized by a black and green band, and a black and green long skirt embroidered with the same Oriental motif as seen on his 'Salome' gown (fig. 16). Like the 'Salome', ropes of pearls adorn the costume.

Poiret's own life was theatrical too. His attraction to fashions based on the Orient extended to a series of lavish fêtes and fancy dress balls which he gave. Here the *beau monde* of Paris wore costumes

24 *Madame Poiret photographed in the costume*
designed by Poiret for her to wear at the '1002nd
Night', 1911. She wears harem pantaloons of
ochre chiffon covered with white chiffon, a short
tunic in gold cloth, wired at the bottom and
edged with a gold fringe, a bodice and sleeves
of chiffon, the sleeves trimmed with fur, and a
turban of gold cloth and chiffon with a large
turquoise and aigrette.

designed by him that became fashions themselves literally overnight. The zenith of his Oriental style was reached when he gave his '1002nd Night' or 'Persian Celebration' in June 1911, attended by some 300 people. Poiret himself played the role of the sultan and Madame Poiret was his 'favourite'. Raoul Dufy and Dunoyer de Segonzac were the artists chosen by Poiret to create the Oriental setting:

I had gathered several artists, and I put my resources at their disposal to realize an ensemble that no one had been able to create before guests. They went up several steps and found themselves in front of an immense golden cage, barred with twisted iron grilles, inside which I had shut up my favourite (Mme Poiret) surrounded by ladies of honour, who sang real Persian airs. Mirrors, sherbert, aquamarines, little birds, chiffons, plumes, such were the distractions of the Queen of the Harem and her ladies of honour.

When my three hundred guests were all present I rose, followed by all my women, went toward the cage of my favourite, to whom I restored her freedoms. She flew out like a bird, and I precipitated myself in pursuit of her, cracking my useless whip. She was lost in the crowd. Did we know, on that evening, that we were rehearsing the drama of our lives.[19]

Georges Lepape made a blissful gouache of Madame Poiret at the moment of release from her cage (frontispiece). Over harem pantaloons she wore a short hooped skirt with a tunic, which the very day after the fête entered the realm of fashion as the lampshade tunic. The atmosphere that was produced by Poiret and his fête in fashionable circles is best conveyed in the words of an eyewitness, Jean Cocteau.

It is a question of being an almeh, a bag of silk and fur, a lamp shade, a cushion from the harem of a fashionable sultan. A pale sultan, an emir with a chestnut beard and protruding eyes, an actor like Nero, changing women into odalisques and capable himself of incarnating innumerable types with the rags that he picks up around him.[20]

The importance of Madame Poiret must be stressed, for she was her husband's inspiration for his creations. It was Madame Poiret, wearing with such *éclat* the costumes designed by Poiret, that led to such rapid copying by those of *bon ton*. A photograph of her dressed for the Persian party shows just how exquisite she was (fig. 24). Her harem pantaloons were made of billowing quantities of white silk chiffon over ochre chiffon and gathered closely at the ankles. Her tunic, held in place by a wide cummerbund, was made of cloth of gold with a gold fringe and was wired along the bottom to create the hooped effect. The bodice and sleeves of the tunic were also of chiffon and the sleeves were trimmed with fur. The sleeves are particularly noteworthy as they were cut in one piece with the bodice and therefore have no seams around the arm socket. They were very wide and created a very deep armhole which almost reaches to the waist, as Madame Poiret's graceful gestures show. Her turban echoed the materials of the garments, being made of cloth of gold wrapped around and held in place by a piece of chiffon and a large turquoise. The turban was surmounted with an aigrette.

The Victoria and Albert Museum is fortunate in having, from Madame Poiret's own collection, the lampshade tunic called the 'Sorbet' (fig. 25). The bodice is formed by kimono-style sleeves cut on the cross. One is in white satin and the other in black satin. They are gathered into a high waistline emphasized by a wide pink silk chiffon sash with a pink fringe. The skirt of the tunic is softly gathered to form a pleat effect and the hem is trimmed with fur and

wired in the same way as the tunic Madame Poiret wore to the '1002nd Night'. This lampshade tunic received the name 'Sorbet' because the glass bead embroidery on the sleeves and skirt is in pink, mauve and green – sorbet or sherbert colours.

It is fitting that the Victoria and Albert Museum should have this outstanding specimen of Poiret's Oriental style because he said in his autobiography that it was his visit to the Museum to see the Indian turban collection that so impressed him and helped him to visualize and then produce his own turbans:

> I visited the South Kensington Museum which is full of the treasures of the Indies. There I found the most precious documents relative to Indian art and manners. In particular there was a collection of turbans that enchanted me. Every kind of way of putting on these headdresses and fixing them on the head was represented. I admired unwaveringly the diversity of their so logical and so elegant forms. There was the little close turban of the sepoys, that ends in a panel negligently thrown over the shoulder; and there was the enormous Rajah's turban, mounted like a gigantic pin-cushion, to receive all the costliest aigrettes and jewels. I at once obtained from the keeper permission to work from these magnificent specimens. I was even allowed to take the turbans from their cases and caress them. I immediately telephoned to Paris for one of my premières. I inspired her with my own flame, and she spent eight days in the

25 'Sorbet' by Paul Poiret, 1912. A lampshade tunic in white and black satin and pink chiffon with glass bead embroidery in pink, mauve and green – the colours of sherbert. The hem is fur-trimmed and is wired to stand away from the body, forming a lampshade effect which Poiret had originally introduced at his '1002nd Night'. The black silk skirt and the necklace are modern replicas.

26 *'Le Collier Nouveau – Robe du soir de Paul Poiret'. Drawn by Georges Lepape, 1914. Another example of the fancy dress of the 'Persian Celebration' translated into fashionable evening wear. The tunic is white, trimmed with fur, and worn over a narrow black velvet evening skirt with a slit up the front to reveal a white silk lining.*

Museum, imitating and copying, reproducing the models she had before her eyes; a few weeks later, we had made turbans the fashion in Paris.[21] While fashionable women revelled in the wearing of Poiret's Oriental fantasies, it was his wife, Denise, who had both the acumen to understand them and the perfect silhouette to wear them. When the editor of *Harper's Bazaar* saw her in one of Poiret's turbans he exclaimed that she had 'a head by Ingres'.[22] This was quite a tribute, for Jean-Auguste-Dominique Ingres was one of the predominant artists of nineteenth-century France. His work was to inspire many modern painters, especially Matisse, during a career which spanned the First Empire of Napoleon I to the Second Empire of Napoleon II. Orientalism was one of the most popular tastes during all of that time. Ingres painted both languid odalisques and fashionable women of French society, rendering them as Oriental Venuses by marrying a classical line to a luxurious tactile pleasure in the colour and texture of textiles, jewellery and fur. It is easy to see why Madame Poiret was identified as an Ingresque type of sensuous ideal.

Madame Poiret's wearing of harem pantaloons was to have a dramatic effect on fashion and also to contribute to a more physical freedom in women's dress, which is usually attributed to the First World War. In January 1911, five months before the 'Persian Celebration', Poiret had launched a collection in which was introduced the 'pantaloon gown'. Other names given to this fashion were the *jupe-culotte*, the 'trouser skirt' and the 'harem skirt'. These outfits consisted of fully proportioned pantaloons or trousers, which fell together to give the appearance of a skirt and were worn beneath tunics. They were included again in his August collection and by October, just a few months after the famous party, Poiret wrote to his wife saying that he was so inundated with

orders that his workrooms were veritable
traffic jams and he and his staff had had to
stay late for three evenings running to
cope with the demand.[23] Although the
pantaloon gown allowed women to walk
properly again and to dance the new craze,
the tango, which required a great deal of
freedom of movement, its appearance at
the racecourse was met with the same
hostile response as the hobble skirt.[24] None
the less, it was not only a fashion which
persisted, but Poiret had anticipated a
whole new trend and would still be
designing pyjamas for day and evening
wear in the 1920s. Georges Lepape
included in his *Les choses de Paul Poiret* a
drawing of four different pantaloon gowns,
perceptively entitled 'Celles de demain',
'Fashions of Tomorrow'. (see plate 4).

As for the lampshade tunic, it was still
being shown in the *Gazette du Bon Ton* as
late as 1914. 'Le collier nouveau – Robe du
soir de Paul Poiret', drawn by Georges
Lepape, shows another version, with a
square-cut bodice and full sleeves
narrowing to a cuff edged with fur (fig. 26).
The sleeves have a series of thin dots
forming a striped pattern. This is repeated
on the tasselled belt which is worn very
high to show off a Directoire waistline.
The black velvet skirt is very narrow but
has a deep slit in front, permitting freedom
of movement and revealing a white silk
lining.

The other leading fashion periodical, the
Journal des Dames et des Modes,
illustrated several fashion plates showing
how other fashion houses had embarked
on variations on Poiret's theme. In 1912,
for example, the *Journal* carried a fashion

*27 **Fashion plate from the** Journal des Dames et
des Modes, **1912. Following the soft and supple
line of Poiret's Orientalism, this fashion plate
shows a gown of black velvet with a double tunic
in black silk muslin, bordered with skunk fur
contrasted with a stole and muff made of white
fox fur. The* Journal *reported a rage for black silk
muslin.***

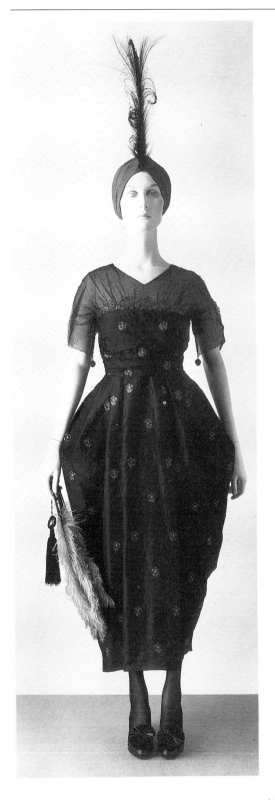

plate of a model wearing a black velvet dress with a two-tiered lampshade tunic of silk muslin trimmed with the skunk fur (fig. 27). She wears a white fox stole draped around her neck and carries a huge white fox muff. The designer was experimenting with the illusion of an ethereal, floating ensemble that Poiret's Orientalism had created. 1912 was the year in which Poiret introduced the white fox stole. Its downy texture was admirably suited to enhance this illusion.

The Victoria and Albert Museum has in its collection an exotic evening dress, dated 1916–17, 'which owes much to Poiret's innovations, especially to his emphasis on Eastern themes'.[25] It is made of black taffeta brocaded with magenta and bright green silks, gilt lace and black net (fig. 28). Vivid colours on a dark background and the contrast of light and dark colours bearing bright, floral motifs was very much a Poiret hallmark (see page 00). The hobble skirt and cummerbund are additional Poiret features retained from the 1910s (see frontispiece, and figs. 12 and 24).

The theatre was a prime source for many of Poiret's fashion innovations in the Oriental style. It was a very exciting time in the theatre. As a fashion designer Poiret benefited a great deal, and he also contributed much to the artistic developments taking place in the theatre. In 1913, the Director of the Théâtre de la Renaissance, impressed by Poiret's costumes and décor for the '1002nd Night', asked him to devise the costumes and sets for a play by Jacques Richepin called *Le Minaret*. Poiret recalled the positive

28 Evening dress, probably French, 1916–17. Black taffeta brocaded with magenta and green silks, gilt lace and black net. The exaggerated draped effect over the hips is due to the skirt being seamed at the centre front and then pleated into a high waistline. The hobble skirt has an elastic strap which is affixed to the centre front and back of the hem.

revolution in the art of stage presentation and design that was effected by *Le Minaret*. It was:

> ... *the first time dress designer and scenic artists had co-operated and had adopted the same conception ... my friends Ronsin, Marc Henri, Laverdet, and I were completely in agreement as to certain very simple dominant harmonies, whose limits we each understood to respect. The first act was to be blue and green. The second, red and violet. The third, black and white. And I did not allow myself a single infraction of this pre-arranged scheme.*[26]

For help with the costumes Poiret called upon the services of Erté, whom he had recently discovered and taken on as an assistant designer. The most successful costume to emerge was that worn by the leading actress, Mata Hari, the Oriental dancer who had been receiving critical acclaim in Paris as well as in other capital cities of Europe.[27] For her a costume was created that was to be translated into fashion as the Minaret gown, but which was really an adaptation of the lampshade tunic (fig. 29). Erté wrote eloquently about it:

> *Throughout 1913, fashion was dominated by the costumes of* The Minaret. *Skirts were draped tightly around the legs, rather like the trousers of Eastern dancing-girls, and belts were wide like oriental sashes. But the main feature of this style was the little tunic-crinoline shaped like a lampshade, inspired by the transparent veils of the Hindu miniatures, and by the pleated kilts (or 'fustanelles') of Greek folk costumes. Romantic fantasies of the East, influenced by Diaghilev's Paris production of* Schéhérazade, *were popular. Poiret's fashions reflected them both in style and choice of colours.*[28]

29 **Poiret's costume design for Mata Hari in** Le Minaret, **1913, drawn by Erté. For this play Poiret also created the 'Minaret' gown, a variation on the lampshade tunic. He gave the hoop some flare, retaining the lampshade shape. To this he added the tiered skirts that he had originally designed for Ida Rubinstein. Poiret made some fantastic and amusing aigrettes to wear with turbans which, nevertheless, lengthened the silhouette as intended.**

47

The bold, stylized floral design, a motif already seen on many Poiret costumes, was spaced with as much geometric precision as, say, the flowers on the 'Sorbet' (see page 43). The harem skirt worn here is slit quite high up at the front of the legs for maximum freedom of movement, and is held in place by jewelled buttons. Erté reiterates that the part of Poiret's Oriental silhouette which caused most scandal were these *jupes-culottes*.[29]

The turban was once again an integral part of the costume and again it was Madame Poiret who provided the fashion stimulus. Erté described her as 'the dazzlingly beautiful Madame Poiret, who looked like a tiny Chinese porcelain figure, with her smooth black hair drawn tightly back'.[30] Poiret himself directly linked her with *Le Minaret* and fashion in his autobiography when he wrote:

> *She was to become one of the queens of Paris. Her appearance in elegant places was noted, and several times produced a real sensation. At the first performance of* Minaret *by Jacques Richepin, she wore on her head a turban – a headdress that had not been seen on any Parisienne since Mme de Staël and, as if to accentuate the provocation to public opinion, this turban was surmounted by an aigrette, which must have been about a foot high.*[31]

In the Directoire period, costumes designed for plays had repercussions beyond the theatre. The same was true with Poiret's work. The *élégantes* of the Directoire aped the creations they saw at the theatre and once again fashionable women energetically embraced Poiret's designs.[32] His artistry was recognized as well. Erté, the main artist working with Poiret during his Oriental phase of these pre-war years, suggested in his autobiography that it was Poiret's use of bright colours for clothes, both inside and outside the theatre, that was so important an aspect of his fashion revolution.[33]

Critics concurred that the production of *Le Minaret* marked a new turn in the development of costume design. It also made a profound impression on artists in its use of colours, and thus influenced future illustration.[34]

1. **'Two Directoire Gowns'** From *Les robes de Paul Poiret racontées par Paul Iribe*, 1908. On the right a green gown spotted with gold which has long sleeves and a cross-over bodice. On the left a short-sleeved gown in a grey, pink and white striped pattern, the high-waistline defined by a braided design in grey, yellow and purple which picks out the tones of the dress, stole and Grecian-type *fillet* in the model's hair. Both the flowing, narrow, angular stole of the model on the left and the border design trimming the dress of the model on the right not only reflect the landscape the models are gazing at through the window but also emphasize the Grecian line of the interior décor and serve to anchor these gowns in their Directoire environment. Paul Iribe, a fashion illustrator, designer and interior decorator, was especially fond of the Directoire era. He designed Directoire-style furniture for the celebrated actress, Mlle Spinelly, for whom Poiret designed many costumes.

2. **'Three Coats'.** From *Les robes de Paul Poiret racontées par Paul Iribe*, 1908. Poiret's Orientalism with its brilliant, bold colours and simplicity of line. Iribe has grouped the figures assymetrically, two models turned away from and one facing the viewer, against an entirely empty background. The large blocks of colour of the coats are left unshaded. The combination of these two techniques was used to focus the attention of the viewer completely on the line and vivid colours of the coats. Iribe's album reflected the quintessential qualities of Poiret's fashions.

3. **'Three Redingotes'.** From *Les robes de Paul Poiret racontées par Paul Iribe*, 1908. *Redingote* is the
French word derived from the English words riding coat. Popular in France from the late eighteenth-
century, the distinguishing features of the high-waisted *redingote* were that it should have the appearance
of being a front-opening dress and be close-fitting with lapels. Poiret has beautifully translated the style
into full-length gowns. The first one, on the left, has the effect of a striped spencer (a short jacket very
popular during the Directoire) and skirt. In the centre with the rows of buttons is the 'Lola Montès' –
Mme Poiret wore an identical gown to the christening of her daughter Rosine in 1906.

4. **'Fashions of Tomorrow'.** From *Les choses de Paul Poiret vues par Georges Lepape*, 1911. At the time of this print trouser outfits were considered fairly *outré* designs but they do serve to illustrate the movement toward a greater physical freedom in women's fashionable dress at such an early date.

5. 'Chez Poiret'.
Print by Georges
Barbier which
appeared on the
cover of *Les Modes*,
April 1912. This
composition
shows two models
of Poiret in a
stylized setting
that is supposed
to represent the
garden of a
particular *hôtel*
that was one of
his fashion houses.
The evening coat
on the right has a
long train which
falls from the
shoulders and folds
back at the sides
like huge wings.
It has an intricate
design
representing a
sinuous, stylized
tree. A similar coat
designed by Poiret
called *Battick* was
photographed by
Edward Steichen
and appeared in
Art et Décoration,
April 1911. The
required headwear
to be worn with
the coat and
equally exotic
dress was the
turban trimmed
with pearls and
surmounted with
an *aigrette*.

LES MODES

G. BARBIER

6. **Evening Mantle** designed by Paul Poiret. From the *Gazette du Bon Ton*, July 1922. This garment shows Poiret's dramatic flair for line, colour and pattern. One of the innovations Poiret brought to fashion was his masterly handling of designs of which this is an outstanding example. It is couture work at its best and something the ready-to-wear industry could not emulate.

7. **The Rose Gown.** Designed by Jacques Doucet, 1913.
The model, depicted by the painter and fashion illustrator,
H. Robert Dammy, wears 'the garden party ensemble' of
Jacques Doucet, the famous couturier under whom Poiret
served a rewarding apprenticeship. Note the similarity in
style and movement of the stole here with the one designed
by Poiret (colour plate 2). Doucet was a generous teacher
and it was through him that Poiret gleaned a knowledge of
some of the main artistic movements; for Doucet had an
outstanding collection of eighteenth-century French art,
modern art, and African sculpture, all important sources of
inspiration for women's fashionable dress.

8. **Brocaded Cut-Velvet Evening Cape** c.1924-25. The
cut-velvet has a flamboyant design of butterflies, bird wings,
stylized fruits and flowerheads in multiple tones of crimson,
pink, grey and yellow and flecked overall in gold, bordered
by rust-coloured velvet.

9. **Beaded Evening Coat** by Paul Poiret, c.1924-28. This is a superb example of Poiret's interpretation of Art Déco which emphasized extravagant surface decoration. To get this effect of graduated beadwork in tones of silver-grey deepening into black, embroiderers in the 1920s used wooden stretchers to keep the material taut. Often several embroiderers worked on a single garment which would still take several weeks to make.

10. **Embroidered Black Wool Coat.** Designed by Paul Poiret, c.1924. The black wool background is delicately embroidered in chain stitch with a Chinese influenced design of a landscape within coiling foliage, waterfalls, cockerels in scarlet and ivory silks, and gold thread. Lined with silk, the coat has no fastenings.

3
THE MARTINES AND DUFY

Within the space of a single year – 1911 – Paul Poiret founded the Martine school and Martine shop, devoted to the decorative arts, and named after one of his daughters; Rosine, a house of perfume, the first of its kind, named after another daughter, and Colin, a paper and packaging workshop. With his friend, the painter Raoul Dufy, he established the Petite Usine or 'Little Factory' for fabric printing. As Madame Deslandres says in her perceptive book on Poiret:

> All that was lacking in such a panorama was a gallery of modern art to introduce his favourite new artists to the public. He managed this at the end of 1911 on the ground floor of one of his outhouses in the faubourg Saint-Honoré, which he delegated to Brabazanges.[1]

At the start of the twentieth century the major trends in interior decoration were being launched at schools in Vienna, Berlin and Munich. Poiret's fashion business took him to these cities where he availed himself of the research going on there:

> I went to all the exhibitions of the decorative arts. It was then that I made the acquaintance of the chiefs of the schools, such as Josef Hoffmann, the creator and Director of the Wiener Werkstätte, Karl Witzmann, M. Muthesius, Wimmer, Bruno Paul and Gustav Klimt.[2]

What Poiret admired about the Wiener Werkstätte was its hand-painted silks and its naturalistic style of design, called *Stylisierung*.[3] In particular he liked the school's floral patterns which were reminiscent of folk art. While he appreciated what the teachers there, and also in Berlin and Munich, had achieved, he was appalled by their ramrod methods. He felt that they stifled their pupils' artistic sensibility by rigidly controlling their designs.

To help him initially in his dream of 'creating a new fashion in decorating and furnishing in France', he called on the services of Madame Sérusier, the wife of the painter Paul Sérusier, one of the founders, along with Maurice Denis, Pierre Bonnard and Edouard Vuillard, of the Nabis. She herself taught the decorative arts in Paris schools and she recommended to Poiret some teenage girls from working-class backgrounds, whom she taught several times a week at his mansion, the Hôtel de la Couture, 107 faubourg Saint-Honoré. When Madame Sérusier gave up the project Poiret did not replace her. He described in his autobiography how he created the Martine school of decorative art:

> I scoured the working-class districts around Paris for little girls of about twelve, who had just finished their schooling. I set aside several rooms in my house for them, and I put them to work copying nature, without any teacher. Naturally, their parents soon discovered they were wasting their time, and I had to promise them stipends and prizes. I rewarded the best designs. Free to do as they liked, I discovered all the freshness and spontaneity of their natures.[4]

Poiret saw his role as essentially one of providing the stimulus for the Martines, as he called the girls. He never restrained them or criticized their work. In this way they were not bound by any empirical rules – only by their own untutored vision:

> Whenever it was possible I had taken them into the country or Zoological Gardens, or into conservatories, where each would do a picture, according to whatever motive pleased her best, and they used to bring back the most charming things. There would be fields of ripe corn, starred with marguerites, poppies, and cornflowers; there were baskets of begonias, masses of hortensias; virgin forests through which spread leaping tigers, all done with an untamed naturalness that I wish I could describe in words. I have kept the collection of their works, and I have pages of touching inspiration, which sometimes approach the prettiest pictures of the douanier Rousseau.
>
> To avoid the necessity of having their designs translated by more or less nonunderstanding workers, I made them learn the craft of tapis au point noué, so that they came to weave with their own hands, straight away without any previous design, carpets whence flowered marvellous blossoms, fresh and living as if they had sprung straight from the earth itself.[5]

Hand-made knotted carpets was a very recherché craft to learn. Short lengths of yarn are knotted to warp threads of a plain woven fabric. The foundation material is woven from wool or silk. The pile is of wool or silk which is then tied to the foundation with knots. The Martines were especially noted for their superb thick-pile carpets and for the use of multicoloured yarns which produced flamboyant floral patterns. An outstanding example is the 'Begonias' carpet of c.1913, a burst of bright, bold reds, pinks, yellows and blues. The begonias theme was one of the most popular of the Martine designs, being used over and over again on wallpapers, cushions, screens and curtains. As for the carpets themselves:

> The Martines caused a revolution in the production of haute laine rugs. Poiret publicized them with an exhibition at the Galeries Brabazanges in his building at 109 faubourg Saint-Honoré.[6]

Another successful floral motif of the Martines, by dint of it being chosen for two important commissions, was 'Dahlias'. The fabric was chosen to cover the seats in the Théâtre Michel in Paris in 1917. Then, in 1921, Poiret used it to upholster the chairs in his theatre, L'Oasis. An open-air theatre, this was delightfully situated in the gardens of his fashion house on the avenue d'Antin (fig. 47).

The Martines also excelled at embroidery, particularly in working with glass beads, for example, as seen on the evening ensemble 'Sorbet' in the collection of the Victoria and Albert Museum (fig. 25).

It is probable that the embroidered design of bold stylized flowers was drawn by one of Poiret's young employees in the School of Decorative Art, 'Martine'. He allowed these girls a fairly free hand and was rewarded with patterns which were remarkable for their 'spontaneity and freshness'.[7]
The girls' love of flowers and the patterns they could achieve were undoubtedly given further stimulation by studying the art of painting on porcelain at Sèvres. This porcelain factory dominated the luxury trade in European ceramics with its floral sprays painted in brilliant colours. The reason Poiret sent the Martines to study there was so that they could come back and decorate by hand the bottles for his house of perfume, Rosine. He capitalized on the new developments in the science of organic chemistry, applying its findings to perfumes. He had set up a laboratory in Paris and a factory for bottling and packaging in Courbevoie, a suburb to the west of Paris. Poiret did not advertise, preferring to send out perfumed Rosine cards to his collections and to distribute fans with the names of the scents on the front and delightful floral designs on the back. As the whole scheme was very original, the decoration on the bottles had to be particularly special.

No couturier before him had thought of linking perfumes and dresses ... As for the perfumes, it seems they were the sumptuous dreams of a poet and each bottle was a work of art, carefully fashioned so as to have complete affinity and be in deep harmony with the perfume it contained.[8]
This idea could be extended to the Martines themselves, for complete harmony, the *tout ensemble*, the whole taken together, was what their work was all about. The response from both the public and artistic circles was immediate and favourable. A mere six months after the school started Poiret opened a shop, also called Martine, located nearby at 83 faubourg Saint-Honoré. With the exception of the furniture, which was designed by the artist Pierre Fauconnet, all the wares sold were designed by the Martines – fabrics to cover the furniture, curtains, wallpapers, screens, printed fabrics, ceramics, embroideries and carpets. Proof of the Martines' acceptance in the art world came in 1912 when the prestigious Salon d'Automne held an exhibition of their designs and textiles. The recognition of the work of the Martines as a new decorative arts movement of international standing came when orders poured in from Gimbel's in New York and branches of Martine were opened in London at 15 Baker Street and, surprisingly, in Berlin.[9]

For fashion, the most revolutionary aspect of the work of the Martines was the diminishing of the differences between dress and furnishing fabrics.

An elegant woman could wear a dress designed by Poiret in a setting from the studios of his Atelier Martine, her dress, curtains and upholstery ... expressing a harmony of design which emanated from the same source.[10]
There are some interesting photographs showing this new concept of a model wearing a dress by Poiret in an interior where the furnishing fabrics were designed by the Martines. Poiret appreciated one so much that he included it in his book *Art et Phynance* (fig. 30). Here Renée, one of Poiret's most exquisite models, sets off her plain cloche, blouse and *jupe-culotte* with a boldly floral-patterned jacket, the whole outfit brilliantly framed by curtains in a pattern very similar to the jacket. The interior is one of the salons in Poiret's new fashion house at 1 Rond-Point des Champs. Poiret, who was keenly interested in fashion photography, must have been very impressed by the photographer Lipnitzki's artistic use of light filtered across the silk of the curtains and embroidery of the

30   *'Une jupe-culotte' by Paul Poiret. Photograph
by Lipnitzki, 1927. This photograph shows how
Poiret had developed with the Martines a close
relationship between dress and interior
decoration. The outfit and the curtains create a
harmony of design, colour and line.*

jacket, both highlighting and interrelating the details of the designs and the textures of the fabrics.

The Martines also undertook commissions to decorate private homes, theatres, restaurants, offices, tea-rooms, hotels and even the luxury steamship, the *Ile-de-France*. One project undertaken by the Martines and Poiret together was for the dancer Isadora Duncan. An American, she was enthusiastically received in London for reviving classical dancing. Wearing Ancient Greek dress, she achieved an appearance very similar to that of the dancers on Greek vases she had studied in the British Museum.[11] She established schools of classical dance in Berlin and Moscow, and was dancing on the stage in Paris in 1907, right at the time Poiret was evolving his Directoire Revival. While dress reformers back in the 1880s and again in the early 1900s advocated the freeing of the body, it was Isadora Duncan in the realm of the dance and Poiret in the realm of fashion who were most successfully developing, refining and promoting it.

Isadora Duncan was a member of Poiret's circle in Paris. *Soirées*, such as Poiret's 'Les Festes de Bacchus' in June 1912, and her 'Souper Grec', also held in 1912, at which Poiret was the star guest, show that there was an interaction of ideas on classical dress. Isadora Duncan was, in fact, one of the most loyal champions of all his fashions.

> *His clothes fitted her idea of the free woman. She wore his Hellenic creations everywhere, ordered the first furs that he showed and after World War I went to Russia wearing knee-high boots provided by him.*[12]

Isadora Duncan was also a staunch supporter of his new ideas in interior design. In her autobiography she described most vividly the decorative innovations to her little apartment and the effect they had on her.

> *But there was a little apartment on the high balcony which had been transformed by the art of Poiret into a veritable domain of Circe. Sable black velvet curtains were reflected on the walls in golden mirrors; a black carpet and a divan with cushions of Oriental textures completed this apartment, the windows of which had been sealed up and the doors of which were strange, Etruscan tomb-like apertures. As Poiret himself said on its completion, 'Voilà des lieux ou on ferait bien d'autres actes et on dirait bien d'autres choses que dans des lieux ordinaires.'*
>
> *This was true. The little room was beautiful, fascinating, and, at the same time, dangerous ... At any rate what Poiret had said was right. In that apartment one felt differently and spoke differently ...*[13]

Many artists were enthusiastic about the work of the Martines and visited them at their school, most notably Raoul Dufy. With his usual perspicacity, Poiret relates in his autobiography why he chose Dufy to participate in his decorative arts movement:

> *We had the same inclination in decoration. His spontaneous and ardent genius had splashed with flowers the green panels of the doors of my dining room in the Pavillon du Butard. We dreamed of dazzling curtains and gowns decorated à la Botticelli. Without counting the cost I gave Dufy who was then making his beginnings in life, the means whereby to realize a few of his dreams. In a few weeks we fixed up a printing workshop in a little place in the Avenue de Clichy, that I had specially hired. We discovered a chemist called Zifferlein, as tiresome as a bushel of fleas, but who knew from top to bottom all about colouring matters, lithographic inks, aniline dyes, fats*

*31 **Design for a fabric by Raoul Dufy, c. 1912–13.**
In this floral design for Bianchini-Férier Dufy has
retained the same naive, primitive look of his
work with Poiret and the Martines.*

*and acids. So here we were, Dufy and
I, like Bouvard and Pecuchet, at the
head of a new craft, from which we
were about to draw new joys and
exaltations.*[14]

Dufy's talent was essentially in the
decorative arts. More successfully than any
other artist, he turned to artistic purpose
the independence of line and colour that
were an almost inevitable effect of the use
of woodcuts on material. As Poiret
explained:

*Dufy drew for me and cut on wood
designs taken from his Bestiary. From*

*them he created sumptuous stuffs, out
of which I have made dresses which
have, I hope, never been destroyed.
Somewhere there must be amateurs
who preserve these relics.*[15]

Dufy achieved highly attractive results
from this double effect of colour and
dressmanship at the Petite Usine where
the Martines were sent by Poiret to work
with him, especially in the application of
colours. They did this using flat wooden
sticks. Dufy and the Martines often
collaborated on specific projects, such as
Poiret's commission of a set of four wall
hangings. Dufy printed them from his
woodblocks and the Martines provided
sketches of designs on the themes of
'Autumn', 'Hunting', 'The Sea' and 'Still Life'.
They also worked together on Poiret's fête
of the '1002nd Night'. Dufy was appointed
in overall charge of the decoration and was
assisted by the artist Dunoyer de Segonzac.
Dufy supervised everything 'down to the
design of the invitation cards, each one
hand-coloured by a Martine girl'.[16]

Dufy was very much *au fait* with the
developments in the decorative arts which
Poiret had witnessed in Austria and
Germany. He travelled to Munich in 1909
with a fellow Fauve, Othon Friesz, with the
specific purpose of studying '*l'art
munchois*'. This was to take Paris by storm
the following year when the Salon
d'Automne hosted the *Exposition des Arts
Décoratifs de Munich*. Dufy's decoration of
the Pavillon du Butard for Poiret, referred
to above, was in the style of '*l'art
munchois*'. The floral designs painted by
Dufy on the panels of the doors, about
which Poiret enthused, were reminiscent
of Bavarian folk art.[17] The Pavillon du
Butard and its decoration were very
important to Poiret. This was the Versailles
hunting lodge of King Louis XV, built by
one of the most celebrated eighteenth-
century French architects, Jacques-Ange
Gabriel. Poiret hired it from 1911 to 1917
for his lavish entertainments, the most

capricious of which was his 'Les Festes de Bacchus', held on 20 June 1912. All the guests were costumed as mythological characters with Poiret himself in the role of an Olympian Jupiter replete with curly hair, beard and buskins.[18] After the bacchanalian feast, the Paris Opéra presented a ballet. The climax to the fête was at dawn when Isadora Duncan 'burst into a final dance, sweeping Jupiter away before those gracious Olympians'.[19] Poiret's extravanganzas at Versailles could be likened to the *menus-plaisirs* of eighteenth-century French kings and Dufy's decorations were a vital part of the whole scheme.

Like the Martines, Dufy had a penchant for floral designs evoking a primitive *naïveté*. Flowers take pride of place in the *oeuvre* of the Martines and also in that of Dufy (fig. 31). Looking at his fabric designs at the superb exhibition, *Raoul Dufy 1877–1953*, held at the Hayward Gallery in London in 1983–4, his favourite flowers were seen to be roses above all, followed by pansies, amaryllis, convolvulus, anemones, marguerites, clematis, peonies, chrysanthemums, dahlias and tulips. Particularly striking was a design of purple and yellow tulips with green stems on a black background. It was a floral design for printing by hand on *satin ondoyant*. Dufy created it at the Petite Usine specially for the Martine shop.[20] Flowers were very important to Dufy. They were, as he put it, 'the natural vehicles of colour … the first motifs'.[21]

Although he continued to collaborate with Poiret, the success of Dufy's work at the Petite Usine led to his employment, between 1912 and 1928, by the great silk firm Bianchini-Férier. The head office was in Lyons where Dufy would go for discussions about the designs. The fabrics themselves were made at the factory located at Tournon, some 80 kilometres (50 miles) from Lyons. He was thus in an excellent position to study at the

renowned Musée Historique des Tissus in Lyons where not only the history of the Lyons silk industry was on display but also a world history of textiles. Such an embarrassment of riches led him to experiment with new themes and concepts. One of his most original designs was of cowrie shells on red and purple geometric squares, dated *c.* 1918–19 (fig. 32). Dufy used the colours in such a way that their interrelationship created space. The provenance for this idea was

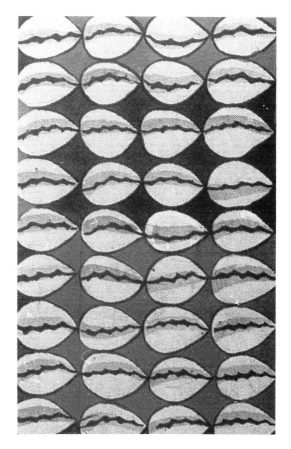

32 *'Cowrie shells on red and purple squares'. Fabric design by Raoul Dufy,* c. *1918–19. Dufy experimented in the abstract use of colour and space derived from Cubism and African textiles. The coloured shapes make their own decorative but formal structure. Dufy's original feeling for line is evident. Poiret chose this design for a silk dress in his summer collection of 1920.*

both old and new, stemming from African textiles and Cubism.

Cubism, which spanned the years *c.* 1907–25, was heavily influenced by African art. It developed from the work of Pablo Picasso and Georges Braque, who sought an intellectual conception of colour and space. The phase called Analytical Cubism (1909–12) excluded bright colours. It was followed by Synthetic Cubism (1912–14) which favoured tactile qualities, and colour became important again. Matisse, who had guided Dufy towards Fauvism, also became preoccupied with Cubism, continuing to use bright colours but juxtaposing them or separating them with white lines. In one design, Dufy has placed cowrie shells on bright, alternating rows of red and purple squares, the juxtaposition of which creates strong, simultaneous spaces. Poiret used this cowrie shells design for a silk dress in his summer collection in 1920. The May 1920 issue of the *Gazette du Bon Ton* illustrated Dufy's *Robes pour l'été, 1920.* Here a group of models parade at the seaside in Poiret creations made from Dufy's many different geometric designs of the period 1918–19 (fig. 6).

While at Bianchini-Férier Dufy found time to write an article entitled 'Les Tissus Imprimés' for the Art Deco journal, *Amour de l'Art* (no. 1, 1920). His views on flowers, noted above, were expressed here. The piece is historically important for several reasons: for the insight it offers into the exciting new developments in fabrics; for the tribute paid to other Fauve painters (Derain had been involved in costume design for the theatre, and Matisse had visited the Martine school and participated in fabric design); and for affirming the interrelationships that had taken place in the arts, with particular reference to painting and fabrics.

The decorative tendency in contemporary painting aided by new methods of manufacture have brought the art of fabric printing to an unparalled degree of perfection ...

Today's printed materials are certainly more beautiful and have more variety than those of other periods because of new methods for treating colours which were unknown to our predecessors. Modern painters, and particularly the group known as the Fauves have offered a precious contribution to the decorative arts: their use of pure colour and arabesque. Their pictures have broken away from their frames to continue on dresses and walls.[22]

The work of the Martines and Dufy heralded the blossoming of the decorative arts in France, culminating in the great *Exposition Internationale des Arts Décoratifs et Industriels Modernes* in 1925. Book illustrations, metalwork, furniture, designs for stained glass, tapestries, ceramic vases and tiles were exhibited, along with costumes and fabric designs which provided another artistic venture for Poiret and Dufy.

One of Dufy's most lush fabric designs was the 'Coquillages et chevaux marin' which he created at Bianchini-Férier in 1922. (fig. 33) This silk is decorated with silver lamé work. The Oriental motifs in sky blue, royal blue and rose reflect the imagery of the woodcuts Dufy executed for Guillaume Appollinaire's *Le Bestiare* of 1911. Rose-coloured horses frolic amongst waves, scallops, dolphins and froth, all spectacularly silver when seen in the light. The critics were dazzled when they saw this fabric made up into a Poiret evening dress and shown on a Siégel and Stockmann display figure at the exhibition.[23]

Poiret's typically original way both to personalize and publicize his contribution as well as that of Dufy, Martine and Rosine at the *Arts Déco* exhibition was to moor three barges on the Seine at the Quai d'Orsay. The official catalogue described them as *Orgues, Amours* and *Délices.*

Orgues was all in white in honour of parades and presented the fashions of the Maison Poiret. *Amours* was decorated in blue carnations by the Maison Martine and presented all the luxurious items made there as well as the perfumes of Rosine. *Délices* was decorated in red anemones by Martine and housed a restaurant. What astonished the critics most were the 14 *tentures* of Dufy. These were wall hangings designed in the Bianchini-Férier factory and made specially to decorate *Orgues.*

> The 'tentures' were composed of three horizontal bands of cotton material dyed in different colours on which Dufy drew in mordant colours. Mordant dyes for cotton were of ancient far eastern origin and were introduced to Europe from Turkey around 1790.[24]

The themes of the *tentures* were the delightful subjects found in Dufy paintings – racecourses, regattas, receptions of the Admiralty and parties at casinos. The most glamorous venue for the fashionable rich to show off their Poiret creations was the racecourse, a veritable extension of the fashion house. As early as 1913 the *Journal des Dames et des Modes* was of the opinion that 'more and more our Parisian racecourses are branches of the showrooms of our great artists of dressmaking'.[25] Dufy is perhaps most famous for his scenes of racecourses and he made a gouache, pencil and collage study of his tenture, 'Les mannequins de Poiret aux courses'. The study, entitled 'Parade des mannequins à Longchamps', concentrates on the fashionable women with tiny horses leaping in the background, as if to emphasize that the racecourse was, in fact, a social fixture where well-dressed women would be seen (fig. 34). This scene confirms the relationship between dress and art and Poiret's view that 'dresses are like pictures. There is only one place where you can put a splash of colour. Here or there is not

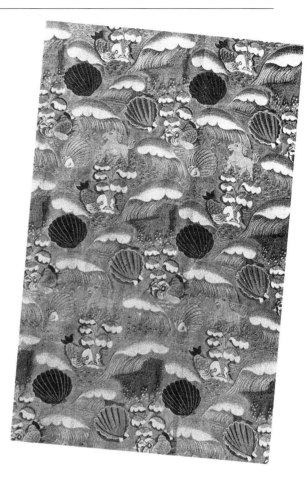

33 **'Coquillages et chevaux marin'. Fabric design by Raoul Dufy, 1922. The delightful way the motifs are counterpointed derives from Dufy's work with woodcuts. The rich silk and silver lamé and the ornamental elements so reminiscent of his** Bestiaire **series of woodcuts exude a** jeux d'esprit. **This fabric was chosen by Poiret for an evening dress displayed at the** Exposition des Arts Décoratifs **in 1925.**

good enough; it has to be precisely placed.'[26]

The dresses, very straight and well above the ankles, are a set of coloured extrapolations of Cubism in its most decorative sense. The lady on the right, for example, wears a white dress with a series of orange-coloured geometric designs on the left of her dress, balanced by a row of large, similarly coloured buttons on the right. The thin black belt around the low waistline is a further sign of geometrical demarcation. It is interesting to note the popularity of a material like chequered gingham acquiring the status of high fashion. A cotton fabric made from dyed yarn, it must have been a refreshing material to wear at the racecourse, especially in the Parisian summer heat. Dufy has cleverly balanced the arrangement of the dresses – dresses that are ornately geometrical in design are always placed next to one in a plain colour with a simpler design. It was with reference to the 'mannequins' that Dufy

34 **'Parade des mannequins à Longchamps' by Raoul Dufy, 1920. Dufy painted a whole series of pictures on the theme of racecourses which he knew well, especially those at Deauville and Longchamps, the setting for this gouache, pencil and collage observation of the Poiret mannequins wearing his smart dresses. A deft calligraphic style is combined with a love of colour and design. Dufy's highly personal pictorial technique was the ideal means for capturing the essence of Poiret's fashions.**

35 and 36 **'La réception à l'Amirauté' and 'La partie de bridge au Casino', by Raoul Dufy, 1925. Two of the fourteen** tentures**, or printed linen wall hangings Dufy made at the Bianchini-Férier factories at Tournon to decorate Poiret's barge,** Orgues**, at the** Arts Déco **exhibition in 1925. It was here that Poiret presented his latest collection. Two of Dufy's** tentures**, 'Les mannequins de Poiret aux courses' and 'Les mannequins de Poiret à la plage' are precious records of some of the late fashions of Poiret. Their collaboration turned the exhibition into a festival of** haute couture **crystallizing the fashions of the period.**

uttered the celebrated words that in his works 'there are colours whose relationships create space'.[27]

The *tentures*, 'La réception à l'Amirauté' and 'La partie de bridge au Casino', afford the opportunity to see examples of evening wear at the time of the *Arts Déco* exhibition (figs. 35 and 36). Dresses tended to be short and sleeveless with the waist at hip level emphasized by a large bow and gathered back drapery. Long hanging drapery attached to the back of the dress and extending into a train seemed to be very popular, as well as the wearing of stoles and the carrying of fans. Materials were either flamboyantly floral or plain, sometimes with the addition of a border design. One revelation is the new type of *décolletage* – backless – usually attributed to the 1930s. It is interesting to observe the male uniforms and fashions and to point out that Poiret was the first couturier to think of designing fashions for men. He had planned to bring out a lavish monthly magazine for men called *Le Prince*. Among those he had chosen to illustrate it were Paul Iribe and Jean-Louis

Boussingault. It is unfortunate that the project was never realized for want of funds.[28]

Poiret and Dufy were at the nadir of their fame; their extraordinary creativity, together with that of the Martines, changed the course of the decorative arts in France. Poiret had achieved what he had originally set out to do. He tried to persuade his business associates at his fashion house to participate in the *Arts Déco* exhibition and to lend him financial support. When they refused, he took on the financial responsibility himself. Writing in *Art et Phynance* in 1934 he recalled:

> *I saw the efforts made by our German neighbours to launch in Europe the novelties characteristic of the spirit of the times. I wanted France to create a movement parallel to the German one in all branches of the luxury industry: furnishing, interior decoration, perfumes, bottles, patterns, carpets, furniture, mirrors, cutlery, lighting, embroidery, trimmings, lace, dresses and coats. That is what I have succeeded in creating.*[29]

4
THE FASHIONS OF POIRET AFTER WWI

Through the work of the Martines and Dufy, some of Poiret's post-war fashions have already been glimpsed. Despite the horrors of the war, shops and salons continued to provide fashionable ladies with stylish clothes. Even during the closing battles of the final year of the war, 'fashion was still a strong influence according to reports in the press'.[1] After the war was over, ladies in the *beau monde* continued to have a vast array of chic clothes for a multitude of occasions – luncheons, dinners, balls, garden parties, races, travelling, walking and the new passion for sport. Resurgence was immediate. The celebrated *Gazette du Bon Ton* (1912–14) was restarted in 1920 and a new magazine was launched called *Art-Goût-Beauté*.

All the *grands couturiers* relaunched their houses after the war, among them Poiret. This phase of Poiret's *oeuvre* is greatly neglected. It is the aim of this chapter to show that while he continued with his pre-war interest in Orientalism, he gave it a new dimension, and also to show that he constantly updated his fashions and that even into the early 1930s he was still active in the world of *haute couture*.

During the First World War Poiret served as a tailor in the army. His first thought on leaving the army was to reopen his fashion house and the Rosine and Martine enterprises. The main activity of the Martines during the war years was the teaching of sewing to soldiers in Normandy.[2] Although there were still some seven Martines by 1917, Poiret decided not to re-establish the Ecole Martine.[3] However, he kept in touch with them and called upon his best pupil, Alice Natter, to provide him with some new designs.[4] When he opened his new fashion house at 1 Rond-Point des Champs-Elysées on 1 January 1925, it was furnished by Martine (see pages 51–3).

After such a protracted absence from the fashion scene, the first collection which Poiret launched, on 1 August 1919, had a very enthusiastic response.[5] A foretaste was given to his faithful client, the Princess Georges Ghika (Liane de Pougy). She was one of the leading members of Parisian society and knew all the great couturiers – Jacques Doucet, Madeleine Vionnet and Coco Chanel. Yet she chose three Poiret dresses to wear to

37 **Cover from American edition of** Vogue, **1 June 1920. Tennis was a popular sport in the 1920s. The queen of the tennis courts was Suzanne Lenglen, who was dressed by the couturier Patou. The tennis player here prefers a Poiretesque Oriental coat as a covering. Tennis dresses generally had a boxy top with narrow shoulder straps and a pleated skirt with a hemline just above the knees. Her companion wears a blue-checked ensemble which has a small white collar and a black scarf tied in a bow. Her hat is in the deep-crowned cloche style, white with blue dots and dashes, with the crown encircled by a blue ribbon band tied in a bow.**

some of the great social events in Paris. The entry in her diary for 25 July 1919 shows that Poiret's taste was distinctly Oriental:

Today we acknowledge that Paul deserved his nickname, the Magnificent. He arrived by car, at midday, surrounded by his boxes, suitcases, his most elegant and favourite mannequin, Germaine his faithful ambassadress (her diplomacy earns her the title), and my vendeuse. Nearly twenty models, each more ravishing than the last ... I chose three dresses: 'Tangiers', in thick black wool with touches of white embroidery and fringed with the same. It's ravishing. 'Saint-Cyr', in black silk, rather full-panniered style skirt, black bodice with short sleeves, and three-overlapping flounces of white organdy making a cape fastened with two silver tassels and a bow of violet velvet. 'Agrigento', two splendid lengths of glitter knotted on the shoulders and at the waist – that's all, but such a ravishing all! He had some superb coats, one of them Venetian, black and gold with a collar and cuffs of sable! 7,500 francs, a mere trifle! But a dream of beauty.[6]

The popularity of Orientalism continued apace after the First World War. On the cover of its issue for 1 June 1920, announcing the summer's fashions, *Vogue* featured a coquettish tennis player enveloped in a Poiretesque Oriental-style coat which he had made so famous before the war (fig. 37). Then, in 1922, interest in the Orient reached fever pitch with the discovery, by Howard Carter and Lord Carnarvon, of Tutankhamun's tomb at Luxor in Egypt. The objects in the tomb were drawn and photographed and had an impact on all art forms.[7]

For Poiret, however, the Eastern theme that he found in 1919 was based on his own experience, which he applied to his fashions with great originality and perception. Princess Georges Ghika mentioned that one of the Poiret dresses she ordered was his 'Tangiers' dress. In his collection it was worn under a majestic cape. The catalyst for this ensemble was a trip to Morocco which he decided to make immediately after leaving the army.

> *I felt I could not get back to work without first resuming contact with some element of pure and revivifying beauty. I was very depressed by military life, and only my robust constitution had saved me from sinking into neurasthenia. On the spur of the moment I decided to spend several weeks in Morocco, before restoring life to my business.*[8]

The 'Tangiers' outfit was drawn by Georges Lepape in the *Gazette du Bon Ton* in February 1920 and given the alluring title, 'Tanger ou les charmes d'exil' ('Tangiers, or the Charms of Exile'). It is representative of Poiret's new interpretation of the East.

> *... to seek inspiration ever more freely from Eastern costumes – ranging very broadly from Persian to Japanese – no longer reproducing a single form exactly, as he had done before 1914 (for example with the 'Hispahan' coat), but rather interpreting its spirit, in creating garments which hung loosely on the body ...*[9]

Both the 'Tangiers' garments were made of Moroccan sackcloth, a heavy, coarse material closer to hemp than canvas. The dress has a round neck with a front opening with fastenings in the form of blue and green wool pompons and is edged with white trim. The skirt is triangular in shape. The cape has white-embroidered seams which form abstract shapes and is decorated with blue wool pompons. When it is taken into account that the 'Tangiers' outfit is now nearly 70 years old, the harmony between fabric and design is truly inspiring.

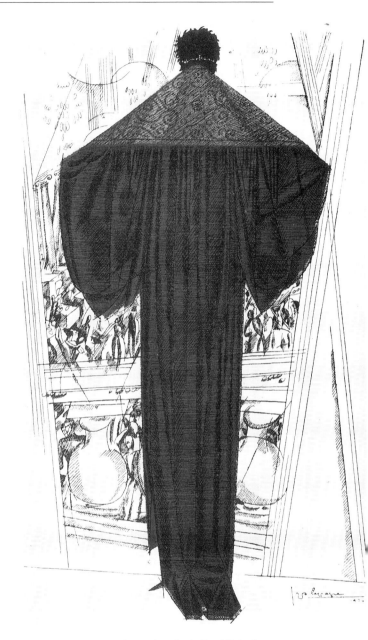

38 'Dancing – Manteau du soir de Paul Poiret'. Drawn by Georges Lepape, 1920. The end of the First World War brought with it a dancing craze. Poiret's Oriental coats, mantles, capes and cloaks turned the dance halls into fashionable occasions. His style now was for the garments to be made in a plain material offset by rich brocade pieces on the shoulders and back.

39 **Evening coat by Paul Poiret. Lithograph by Raoul Dufy, 1920. The** Gazette du Bon Ton **for January/February 1920, the first number to appear after the end of the First World War, was issued with a supplement containing a set of eight lithographs by Dufy. All the models wear Bianchini-Férier fabrics designed by Dufy and made up into Poiret creations. They were all roughly sketched by Dufy and, as this one shows, provided a contrast in style to the** Gazette du Bon Ton **which was dominated by** pochoir **illustrations.**

But Poiret's Orient continued to include the coats, capes, cloaks and mantles of his pre-war years, concentrating now on the decorative features begun with his 'Hispahan' coat. He produced the most sublime collar, shoulder and back effects. The *Gazette du Bon Ton* featured a number of enchanting back views. Georges Lepape's 'Dancing – Manteau du soir de Paul Poiret' appeared in the March 1920 issue (fig. 38). A stunning piece of brocade envelops the shoulders and extends to the huge, billowing sleeves. The stylized floral pattern is typically Poiret. One of the most significant innovations that Poiret brought to the world of fashion was his skill in working with patterned fabric. In this particular example it is not surprising to find a strong, artistic link, again with Raoul Dufy. The January/February 1920 number of the *Gazette du Bon Ton*, the first issue to appear after the First World War, had appended to it a folder which contained a set of drawings by Dufy showing mannequins wearing garments designed by Poiret and made up in Bianchini-Férier materials designed by Dufy.[10] Among the items in the folder was a *croquis* of the evening coat described above (fig. 39). It shows Dufy's distinctive calligraphic draughtsmanship, the rapid hatching brilliantly evoking the Oriental quality of the coat with its Persian-like brocade piece, as well as offering a contrast in fashion-illustration technique to the *pochoir* illustration of Lepape.

In 1922 the *Gazette du Bon Ton* included a drawing by André Marty of an even more riveting back view of an evening mantle in cream and red velvet with a pattern of stylized leaves, branches and fruit in tones of red, cream and grey. This should be borne in mind when looking at one of the items in the sale of the great costume collection of Mary Vaudoyer, held at Sotheby's in Monaco in 1987. This was a brocaded cut-velvet evening cape, dated *c.* 1924–5, with no

identification as to the couturier.[11] It is so
similar in feeling to the mantle in the
Gazette du Bon Ton that there seems to
be a strong case for bearing Poiret in mind
(see plate 8). The cut-velvet brocade has
an arresting design of stylized leaves,
branches, fruits, flower-heads, butterflies
and birds' wings in colours of crimson,
pink, green and yellow, flecked overall
with gold and bordered by rust-coloured
velvet, added to which is a delightful tassel
made up of the multitudinous tones of the
design. There are all the hallmarks of
Poiret. Another mantle in the Vaudoyer
sale, of rose-pink velvet, dated *c.* 1924, was
'attributed to Poiret'.[12] It bears comparison
with the mantle dated *c.* 1913 discussed
earlier (fig. 18). It is draped in the same
way to the body at hip level and fastened
with a large pink silk rose, the
unmistakable Poiret symbol (fig. 40).

Poiret's Orientalism was considerably
updated through the widespread wearing
of pyjamas. In Chapter 2 it was pointed out
that long before the First World War Poiret
had not failed to grasp that the movement
toward them was already underway. It was
a garment that crossed the threshold from
evening wear into day wear. In 1924 'Satin
is used for evening for the first time –
Poiret's poppy and cornflower prints make
evening pyjamas that look particularly
good with the brief bobbed hair.'[13]

Poiret's Orientalism was still thriving as
late as 1926. Princess Georges Ghika
described the imagery she saw at a
luncheon at the Lido:

At the lunch the women, more
coquettish, looked as though they were
acting in a fairy-tale: Schérérazade,
Salomé, Salammbó – oriental ladies

40 *Rose-pink velvet mantle, attributed to*
Paul Poiret, c. 1924. A beautiful simple
fashion statement on line
and colour. An interesting
detail on this mantle is the
drawn threadwork decoration.

from rich harems. They went by in sumptuous pyjamas of silk or figured velvet, brilliantly coloured, glittering with sequins and stones. Fantasy reigned, at its wildest.[14]

Poiret was fully aware of the new trend towards a more practical style of dress – 'even Poiret makes sports jumpers and pleated skirts'.[15] The jumper and pleated skirt seemed to be part of the garb of every woman. As these garments emphasized the long, streamlined look, it is easy to see why Poiret designed them. He created a number of fashions for afternoon wear, with a silhouette that was simple and uncluttered, and he also travelled to publicize them more widely. This included a visit to the United States in 1922 (his first fashion tour had been in 1913), seeing the New World, with the consequences of the war, as the prime source of sales. He was also determined to make contact with provincial centres in Europe 'where women who were unaccustomed to patronizing Paris fashion houses represented a huge untapped market'.[16]

To this end, one of his most distinctive statements of style was a two-piece afternoon dress in faille dated *c.* 1919–22 (fig. 41). The top is ingenious as well as practical for it is basically in the form of a handkerchief with four corners, which simply goes over the head and can then be arranged in any way the wearer wishes. Up until 1924 the length of the skirt fluctuated, 'but always around ankle to mid-calf'.[17] The skirt of this ensemble is straight and very slim, reminiscent of a sarong. Given the Oriental overtones of this dress the headscarf is aptly shaped like

41 Two-piece faille afternoon dress by Paul Poiret, 1919–22. Poiret revived the wearing of faille, a material much used in the late nineteenth century but now almost forgotten. The fabric has a clinging quality which was used to advantage here to obtain the slim, sarong-shape of the skirt.

a turban. Having a colour scheme of red and navy, the outfit was called the 'July 14 Dress', the patriotic aspects of Parisian fashion being increasingly emphasized in the immediate post-war years. There is a certain timelessness about this dress. Diana Vreeland, in her book *Inventive Paris Clothes 1909–1939*, written in 1977, said that it is 'a Poiret that could easily be made and worn today'.[18]

Another dress, purchased by Princess Georges Ghika, would probably also fit into the category of agelessness. In her diary for 15 October 1919 she mentioned that, 'Happily I was wearing a pretty Poiret dress, two years old, but Poiret is always up to date ... a long dress of off-white bouclé wool.[19]

A grey crêpe de Chine afternoon dress, dated *c.* 1923–4, from the Mary Vaudoyer Collection, was assigned as 'possibly by Poiret' in the Sotheby catalogue of the sale.[20] It is straight and loose-fitting, with the waistline now dropped to the level of the hips and the hemline at mid-calf. Poiret attributes are the wide sleeves cut in one with the bodice, with no seam around the arm socket. They are called Magyar sleeves and have drawn threadwork decoration. Most distinctive of all, however, is the coral and white beading on the front and back of the dress, forming bands of the stylized floral patterns he so loved.

Simple but modish and especially interesting is Poiret's day dress 'Brique', dated 1924 (fig. 42). Although the dress is narrow it looks much fuller due to the domination of gathered pockets. It is made of orange worsted flecked with cream,

42 'Brique' day dress by Paul Poiret, 1924. A rather plain dress deftly animated by the application of black-and-white stripes of braid and little tassels. Poiret has cleverly arranged the braid in an assymetrical way across one side of the bodice to enliven the dress further. Note the way the sleeves are set in low, just above the waist, and are very narrow in the arms.

which is considerably animated by the trimmings of black-and-white braid and tassels. Here is a rare example of Poiret experimenting with a manmade fibre, for the braid is made of rayon. The biggest boost to the manufacture of fashions on a massive scale in factories was made by the discovery of the artificial silk called rayon. It came into widespread use in the 1920s, with the United States in the vanguard and Europe following.[21] It meant that millions of less wealthy women could now be in fashion. In the world of *haute couture*, however, dresses were not made of rayon but of the real thing. The *grands couturiers* would use rayon only for trimmings such as braid.

> *Braid manufacturers were among the first bulk buyers of artificial silk and were then joined by hosiery and underwear. Only in the 1930s were couturiers attracted to newly available sophisticated rayon dress goods.*[22]

The workmanship in the 'Brique' is said to be less than ideal as the hem is held down with cotton tape, which apparently was the case with many of Poiret's clothes.[23]

Poiret also produced a new range of coats for day and evening wear. A luxurious summer travelling coat of ivory cashmere twill was woven with *ombré* floral patterns in brown. It has a high standing collar, also with floral patterns (fig. 43). Dated 1919–20 it was an essential part of the wardrobe of a lady of high fashion. Her summer weekends would include motoring, cycling, swimming and tennis. *Vogue* called its issue for 1 June 1920 'Summer Fashions Number' and in this could be found listed and illustrated what the fashionable lady needed for her summer weekends (see page 62). Poiret's love of whimsical touches was evident in his 'Ballon' travelling coat which he designed *c.* 1920. He combined taffeta in hues of blue and grey with black velvet and simulated tortoise skin – a whole new departure for *haute couture* coats.[24]

Poiret's supreme talent in mastering another technique revealed itself in a daytime coat he designed in 1919–20 (fig. 44). It is made of a black ribbed silk and wool mixture and has a collar of white fur that rises to the chin. It is deftly trimmed with latticed bands of white leather cutwork. The patterns Poiret has created are very lace-like. In the sixteenth century cutwork was a form of embroidered lace 'which in its simplest form consisted of holes cut in linen, embroidered around with thread and decorated with buttonhole-stitch bars'.[25] This coat demonstrates Poiret's innate ability to achieve a harmonious interpretation of another of the decorative arts.

It is fortunate that photographs exist showing Poiret with his tailor, M. Christian, meticulously supervising a fitting on one of his models. Poiret always worked on a live model. One particulary interesting photograph of *c.* 1924 shows him with a model and M. Christian making adjustments on a coat which has shoulder tabs and a large fur collar (fig. 45). What strikes one immediately is that the coat shows Poiret as a moulder of fabric *par excellence* in the delightful detail of scalloping on the lapels of the coat. It is pure Poiret.

To Poiret 'nothing was as important as the little piece of poetry that completes the line – the hat'.[26] The hat that dominated the 1920s was the cloche. Taking its name from the French word for bell, it was a small hat with a deep crown, which fitted close to the head. Often referred to as the 'tyrant of the mode', its neat, trim look was achieved by the short, flat hairstyles of the 1920s.[27] The model in the photograph wears a cloche with a brim (they could also be brimless). It is made of black felt and trimmed with strips of white faille. Poiret sought inspiration for his cloche hats from some of his former pupils. For models he called upon

43 *Travelling coat by Paul Poiret, 1919–20. In ivory cashmere, this coat is straight cut with a darker woven floral pattern.*

44 *Daytime coat by Paul Poiret, 1919–20. A black-ribbed daytime coat, a silk and wool mixture, exquisitely trimmed with latticed bands of white leather cutwork and surmounted with a collar of white fur which stands up to the chin.*

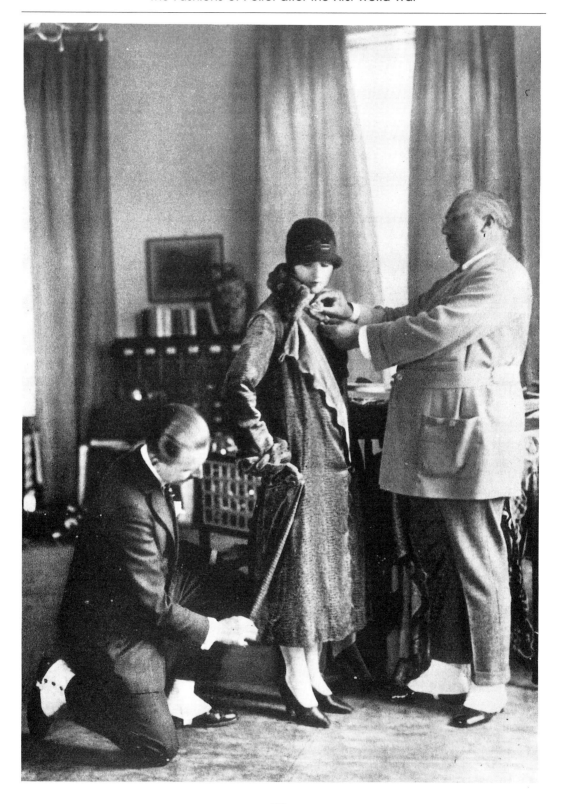

Madeleine Panizon who was one of the great milliners of the period. Sketches of her models were provided by Alice Natter, whom Poiret always considered to be his star pupil at the Ecole Martine. Together the two artists experimented with the line of the cloche and with the materials and colours which best complemented Poiret's creations. Their collaboration included designs for many other hats as well.[28]

During his late period Poiret designed an evening coat that must rank as one of the great masterpieces of the Art Déco style. It was owned by Mary Vaudoyer and included in the Sotheby sale at Monaco. Mary Vaudoyer was a remarkable Scottish lady who made her home in Paris where she collected costume over a period of 40 years. The contents of her collection thus reflected her own interest and tastes: 'the shimmer of colour and light ... perhaps best exemplified by the Poiret coat'.[29] Described in the catalogue as 'fine' and

*45 (left) **Poiret supervising a fitting with his tailor M. Christian**, c. **1924**. This photograph affords the opportunity to see some male fashions and hairstyles. Both Poiret and M. Christian wear their hair short and they are clean-shaven. M. Christian wears a suit and Poiret a working jacket. Their shirts have turned-down collars and their trousers are tapered with narrow turn-ups. The centre crease is pronounced. They both wear spats, a covering for the ankle made of canvas, fastened with buttons on the outer side and with a strap passing under the foot.*

*46 (right) **Evening gown of ivory satin with jade-green velvet trimming by Paul Poiret, 1933**. The front has a cowl neckline, the satin softly draped and falling across the bodice in a loose semi-circle, with a small inner, covered weight to keep the draped-effect. The jade-green velvet trimming on the sides of the bodice extends at the back into a ripple of ribbons. This evening gown was one of a number of designs Poiret was commissioned to do for Liberty's Model Gown Salon. His connection with the store went back to 1909 when, on a visit to London, he purchased Liberty fabrics which he made up into summer dresses.*

'rare', it is dated *c.* 1924–8.[30] It is entirely beaded by hand in hues of silver-grey graduating into black (see plate 9). Poiret here makes a final statement of his beloved kimono-style, reflected in the sleeves and the loose, easy-to-wear shape, emphasized in the front by the simple button fastened to one hip.

Poiret produced these magnificent creations in the 1920s under great financial adversity. By the 1930s he was virtually bankrupt, yet he declared: 'I feel I have many more dresses in me'.[31] The early 1930s were dominated by a new diagonal line of dress. This was achieved by the bias cut, cutting the material of the dress on the grain. The bias cut gave the couturier more scope for moulding and draping the fabric, which has a much more elastic quality when cut on the diagonal. Happily, this new silhouette coincided with a general revival of interest in classical art, for the bias-cut dress epitomized again the soft, supple draperies of ancient Greek sculpture. It is a style that suited Poiret who had created such elegant dresses during his Directoire Revival period. In 1933, Liberty of London commissioned Poiret to design a collection for their Model Gown Salon. One stunning evening gown that survives shows once more his superb workmanship and fluid lines (fig. 46). It is made in bias-cut ivory satin and trimmed with jade-green velvet. Distinctive Poiret hallmarks are the vertical gathers at the midriff, echoed by the exquisite pleating in the skirt. The critics enthused over Poiret's collection for Liberty, writing that he had 'lost none of his striking originality and individuality'.[32]

5

POIRET, ARTISTS AND PHOTOGRAPHERS

Poiret was an endlessly creative couturier whose late work received much critical acclaim. However, like all great artists with original minds, there was an urge to self-destruction. Poiret had no self-discipline and was profligate with the vast amount of money his fashions earned. When it came to managing his financial affairs he was hopelsss. Consequently, in 1924 his fashion house was put in the hands of a board of directors, and later closed in the financial crash of 1929. His Martine and Rosine enterprises were sold in 1926 and disappeared in the same financial crash. Together with impoverishment came ill-health and the break-up of his marriage with the beautiful Denise. His last years were spent painting. An exhibition of his paintings was held at the prestigious Galerie Charpentier in Paris in 1944, the year of his death. This was a fitting tribute; Poiret's mission had always been fashion nourished by artists.

The organizers of the 1925 *Arts Deco* exhibition had publicly acknowledged the debt owed to Poiret by the modern decorative arts movement in France. He made textile design fashionable and his work with Raoul Dufy, featured at the exhibition, served to highlight the superiority of French textile design. The leading firms at the two great French centres, Lyons and Mulhouse, were way ahead of firms in other countries in the manufacture of decorative textiles specifically designated for couturiers in Paris. Their pattern books and samples exist today at the Musée Historique des Tissus in Lyons and the Musée de l'Impression sur Etoffes in Mulhouse. They comprise the work of many artists, but the foundations being laid by Poiret and Dufy.

> *Practically all modern fabric design, internationally, was first formulated by Dufy … at first for Paul Poiret's dresses which founded the modern shape and style and opened the door for Chanel and Schiaparelli, and then for the great Maison Bianchini-Férier in Lyons.*[1]

Another area towards which Poiret had directed his artistic energies was the production of extremely fine illustrations for almanacs and albums that harked back to historical sources. In 1917 Martine published his *Almanach des Lettres et des Arts*. The purpose of the *Almanach* had

47 'At the Oasis, under the pneumatic dome'.
Evening gown by Paul Poiret. Drawn by André
Marty, 1921. 'L'Oasis' was a theatre in the garden
of Poiret's fashion house. With his usual artistry,
he presented a wide variety of entertainments,
ranging from recitals by Yvonne Guilbert to
revivals of plays and an array of fêtes. The model
wears a Poiret creation consisting of a red crêpe
tunic and a shimmering gold skirt. An exquisite
detail is the embroidery of golden ears of corn.
The chairs are upholstered in a Martine fabric.

been to publicize the perfumes of Rosine. Poiret assigned overall artistic supervision to Raoul Dufy in the light of his magnificent woodcuts for Apollinaire's *Le Bestiaire* of 1911, but also sought the participation of other artists, notably Jean-Louis Boussingault and Jean-Émile Laboureur. Among the items in the volume were a calendar and anthology with woodcuts by Dufy illustrating poems by La Fontaine, Ronsard, Villon, Mallarmé and Rimbaud. It was a timeless theme 'within the French tradition to the *Très Belles Heures du Duc de Berry*'.[2] There was an artistic resurgence in book illustration, many of them masterpieces of contemporary design.[3] They were sought after by the high-class Art Déco periodicals, especially the work of Dufy, whose illustrations for *La Terre Frottée d'Ail* appeared in 1925.[4] In 1928 Poiret published *Pan*, an album designed to advertise French luxury products. To obtain freshness of vision he particularly sought out drawings by artists who had not worked before in the field of commercial illustration. As with the earlier albums produced by Iribe and Lepape, Poiret insisted on a luxury edition using high-quality paper and a superb layout. Among the items were the work of the *couturière* Madeleine Vionnet and the photographer Lipnitzki.[5]

So innovative was Poiret that the exhibition held at the Musée Jacquemart–André in Paris in 1974, *Poiret, le magnifique*, had a whole section entitled 'L'ami des artistes', where it was shown that as late as 1931 Poiret collaborated with the artist Kees Van Dongen on a brochure called *Deauville*. Commissioned by the owner of the Casino de Deauville, Poiret wrote the text and Van Dongen provided the illustrations.[6] After the racecourse, the casino was probably the best place to view the latest fashions. Undoubtedly with this in mind, the casino was the venue once chosen for models to display some of the costumes in the collection of Mary Vaudoyer.

In spite of his own personal difficulties Poiret continued to maintain an active interest in all the arts and to encourage further new developments in them, especially in fashion illustration and photography. Fashion illustration was still the avenue for forging the closest relationship between the couturier who clothed the fashionable lady with fabric and the artist who did so with stencils and paints. The *Gazette du Bon Ton* depicted many of Poiret's costumes in his own settings, which demonstrate a complexity of style in both fashion and the illustration of it. André Marty had been one of the first artists to draw the fashions of Poiret in the *Gazette du Bon Ton* when it was founded. After the First World War, he not only drew his fashions but placed them within intricate settings. The scene for one of his fashion plates for the *Gazette* in 1921 is Poiret's theatre, L'Oasis. (fig. 47) It had opened in 1919 as an outdoor summer nightclub in the gardens of his fashion house. In the summers of 1920 and 1921, however, Poiret turned it into a theatre. With his usual flair for art and history, Poiret studied French literature and drama and then designed the costumes and sets himself.[7] Among those who performed there was Yvonne Guilbert, celebrated in the graphic work of Henri de Toulouse-Lautrec.

Marty was also a literary critic and his speciality was writing reviews of modern dance. He fused his knowledge of fashion and dance with the techniques of perspective seen previously in painting, but hitherto not explored in fashion illustration. In 'At the Oasis', Marty has adjusted the viewer's angle to the flat picture plane and his distance from it by his use, in the foreground, of elegantly dressed curvilinear figures on the left, tilting the scene slightly upwards as they look up at the spectacular dome made of airship cloth which is golden yellow in the evening light. The middle ground is grid-like with the audience sitting in cubic-shaped chairs by the Martines, upholstered in their 'Dahlias' fabric. The background, with its airy height of dome and stage, opens out onto the evening landscape, becoming a backdrop in the true theatrical sense. There is a great deal of life and movement in the scene as the many varied stances of the dancers contrast with those of the foreground figures, particularly the graceful model who is echoed by the curving lines of her off-the-shoulder tunic.

Another artist to whom Poiret gave his support was Pierre Brissaud. Brissaud had won critical acclaim at the Salon des Indépendants along with Jean-Louis Boussingault and had also exhibited his work at the Salon d'Automne in 1907.[8] He belonged, along with André Marty, Georges Barbier, Charles Martin, Paul Iribe and Georges Lepape, to the original group of artists who contributed to the *Gazette du Bon Ton* at its inception. Edna Woolman Chase, who knew them all, said they called themselves Beaux Brummells or the Knights of the Bracelet.

A certain dandyism of dress and manner which is a constant characteristic of a group makes them a 'school'. Their hat brims are a wee bit broader than the modish ones of the day and the hats are worn with a slight tilt, a very slight tilt but enough to give the impression of fastidiousness. Their coats are pinched in just a little at the waist, their ties are spotless and their boots immaculate. A bracelet slipping down over a wrist at an unexpected moment betrays a love of luxury.

The great difference between these Beaux Brummells and their ancient namesake is that, while they are thoroughly imbued with same love of

48   *'Soleil d'hiver'. Watercolour by Pierre
Brissaud, 1924. Skating, or at least its romantic
aspects, was a favourite activity for the
fashionable lady. This skating outfit is very
Poiretesque, with loads of fur, elaborate clasps
and tassels on the coat. The cloche hat is pulled
well down and fits her head very snugly.*

76

elegance and luxury, they are also hard and vigorous workers.[9]
Besides his drawings of Poiret's fashions for the *Gazette du Bon Ton*, Brissaud also produced an independent series of watercolours. In these it is precisely this contemporary dandyism that he captures (fig. 48). He does this through humour and was one of the first artists to use wit to convey the mood of a woman's costume. His scenes are always full of narrative and in this delightful and amusing skating scene, where the two dandies in tandem ogle the fashionable lady, the spectator can imagine the seeds of a story.

Poiret also took an avid interest in a whole new generation of artists. In July 1916, at his Galerie Barbazanges, he staged an exhibition of the works of young, avant-garde artists under the title 'Salon d'Antin: L'Art Moderne en France'. In 1923, when an exhibition of his private collection was held in the same gallery, André Salmon, the leader of the Surrealist artists, acknowledged their debt to Poiret, saying that he had 'put an end to the many powerful forces hostile to modern art'.[10]

One new artist, whose talent Poiret immediately spotted, was a Spaniard called Eduardo Garcia Benito, who styled himself Benito. His drawings of Poiret's fashions for the *Gazette du Bon Ton* in the period 1920–2 were so highly thought of that they were included in a two-volume publication of fashion plates called *Le Bon Ton d'après Guerre*. Yet there is a dearth of information about Benito. It is hard to find an entry on him in biographical directories of artists or to find him mentioned in studies of Poiret or general fashion histories of the period. His main attribute in fashion illustration was the extreme elongation of the figure of the model (fig. 49), very reminiscent of sixteenth-century Spanish Mannerist painting. Benito would also have been influenced by Cubism and the *Exposition Nationale Coloniale de Marseille* of 1922,

49 *Afternoon dress by Paul Poiret. Drawn by Edouardo Benito, 1922. A black crêpe afternoon dress with white trim, worn with a narrow black-and-white crêpe stole with tassels and a black-and-white picture hat. Benito's extremely elongated figure was perfect for emphasizing the line of Poiret's creation – straight from shoulder to hem with the line broken only by the detail of the gold trim at hip level to accentuate the low waist. In her hand the model holds a white vanity case with a jade-green tassel. The vanity case evolved from the need of the fashionable lady to carry her make-up and other indispensable items. It successfully implemented the shapes and motifs of Art Deco fashion.*

featuring African sculpture which also exaggerated the human form.

Another artist whom Poiret patronized was Kees Van Dongen. Although Van Dongen is well known today and his career is well documented, his work with Poiret is little known and deserves more attention. They were great personal friends and Poiret collected Van Dongen's paintings. Van Dongen often visited the Ecole Martine and purchased many of the works of the Martines.[11] Besides their joint venture for the Casino de Deauville, Van Dongen painted many outstanding portraits of well-known fashionable women, which epitomize the feeling of the mid 1920s.[12] In addition, a number of Poiret models came to his *atelier* to be painted in his fashions.[13] 'La Dame en Noir' is one of the outstanding paintings in this group (fig. 51). Exhibited at the Salon des Tuileries in 1924, its importance as a valuable document of fashion is attested to by the fact that it was featured in the *Gazette du Bon Ton* in its July/August number of 1924. Unlike some of the other avant-garde artists whose works Poiret collected, such as Modigliani, Picasso and Picabia, Van Dongen was not concerned to find new ways of representation. 'He was content to place his figures on a bare background … forms are simplified, but he avoid altering them too much.'[14]

Van Dongen specialized in painting full-length figures of women placed close to the spectator. What he loved to do, something which would have received the approbation of Poiret, was to exploit his favourite fashion accessory, the hat. His treatment differed markedly from his fellow Fauve, Matisse.

> *Here too one thinks of Matisse, and the role played by hair arrangement in his* Women with Hat, *although it is in keeping with the fashion of the time, it is scarcely more than a complex of colours and forms. In Van Dongen, on the other hand, the hat acts first and foremost as an adornment or a means of revealing the face and nature of the wearer.*[15]

In this painting the large, wide-brimmed picture hat seems to suggest the worldly, bizarre, even slightly brazen nature of the fashionable lady. Through her hat, Van Dongen gets behind what makes her a *female fatale*. Fashion captured through the lens had always been a preoccupation of Poiret's (see pages 24, 51–3). In 1988, an exhibition held at the Musée des Arts Décoratifs in Paris, entitled *Créateurs de Mode, Créateurs d'Image*, while bereft of any chronological or historical development, had as its central theme the relationship between the couturiers and the photographers they choose as their image makers. Poiret seemed to want not only to record his fashions but, through them, to suggest a life beyond the frame. In this category must surely belong Delphi's photograph of Denise Poiret entitled 'Faune', dated 1919 (fig. 50). Madame Poiret wears a gown which Poiret designed specially for her to wear at 'L'Oasis'. It consists of a gold lamé bodice with a V-shaped opening on the back which is cut down to the waist and has a rolled halter-neck. The skirt is made of imitation monkey-fur fabric, a very popular material during the 1920s, with a gold fringe. She wears gold shoes. Behind her a crucial element in the photograph is Brancusi's brass sculpture called 'Bird in Space'. Constantin Brancusi was a Romanian sculptor who worked in Paris from 1904, producing simple, highly polished pieces. He was influenced by Modigliani, and Poiret collected the works of both. The photographer has deftly posed Madame Poiret against 'Bird in Space'. Indeed, Madame Poiret's bird-like frame, her spiky hairstyle, the fine pleating on her gold lamé bodice and the feathery texture of her skirt all, in one way or another, reflect the bird behind her. It illustrates the direct rapport between Poiret the

couturier and Delphi the photographer as accomplices in style – for Madame Poiret is the ultimate *femme fatale*.

Poiret's last notable collaboration was with the American painter and photographer Man Ray. A Dadaist, Man Ray worked in New York until 1921 when he went, penurious, to Paris. His paintings were included in the first Surrealist exhibition, held in 1925. In his autobiography he recalled the time he went seeking photographic work at La Maison Poiret. For a start the atmosphere of the fashion house suited him:

> *On the walls ... were works by contemporary painters, and on a pedestal in the centre a magnificent gold bird by Brancusi. This different*

50 **'Faune'. Evening gown by Paul Poiret, worn by Madame Poiret, 1919. Poiret designed this exotic evening gown especially for his wife to wear at 'L'Oasis', the postwar venue for his lavish entertainments. It consists of a gold lamé bodice and a skirt made of extravagantly layered monkey-fur fabric and gold fringe.**

atmosphere reassured me; it was more in keeping with my world.[16]

As for meeting the master himself, Man Ray gives the costume historian an interesting account of the assignment Poiret gave him for his summer collection in 1922:

A slight expression of impatience crossed his face; he asked whether I had ever done fashion photographs. I was afraid of this, admitted that I hadn't but hastened to add that I should like to try, it was difficult because I had no studio. With an inclusive gesture, he pointed out that here was his house, the rooms, the dresses, the girls – photographers generally worked on the spot, which he preferred ... He'd like to get some original pictures of his mannequins and gowns, something different, not like the stuff turned out by the usual fashion photographers. He would speak to the mannequins, impress upon them that this work was not the ordinary showing of gowns, but portraiture as well, giving more human qualities to the picture.[17]

Man Ray gives one very vivid description which, not surprisingly, involved the salon in Poiret's fashion house containing the Brancusi sculpture:

The model came out wearing a close-fitting gown in gold-shot brocade, gathered round the ankles in the hobble skirt style of today ... The room upstairs was flooded with sunlight from the windows; I would not need any other light. I had her stand near the Brancusi sculpture, which threw off beams of golden light, blending with the colours of the dress. This was to be the picture I decided; I'd combine art and fashion ... And my model was being very co-operative; she deserved the best I was capable of. I made a couple of exposures; with the good light there could be no doubt about the results.[18]

Everything that Poiret could possibly have wanted was combined and related: brilliant colour, economy of line, definition of textures, portraiture. In making his prints for Poiret, Man Ray hit upon what he called his Rayograph process, or camera-less photography, truly making the camera an artist's tool as pliable as a paintbrush or drawing pencil. 'His "rayographs" which reproduce the effect of a photograph being sent by radio waves, illustrate his dictum that "inspiration, not information, is the force that binds all creative arts".'[19]

Poiret was the first to appreciate Man Ray's Rayographs which quickly gained universal recognition.[20]

In 1921 Man Ray went to Paris and made his first Rayograph, in 1922 he photographed a model at Poiret's salon, and for the next fifteen years the world of culture and fashion were never to be equalled or rivalled for their profound influence on one another.[21]

The commission he gave to Man Ray, and his support of the innovative results, were further superb examples of Poiret's imagination and creativity applied to another art form so important to fashion.

CONCLUSION

While Poiret was transforming women's dress and relating fashion to the arts, he was also working indefatigably to enhance the status of the couturier and to further the development of fashion as an industry.

> *If, to use Poiret's own expression, the 'great Worth' was the founder of the Haute Couture industry, it was Poiret himself who redefined and fundamentally changed its rules, practices and methods.*[1]

So many of his ideas seem very logical today but were unheard of at the time. He founded the first house of perfume, Rosine, 'more than ten years before Chanel and nearly fifteen years before Lanvin'.[2] Moreover, he provided a direct link between his scents and his fashions. The bottle for his fragrance 'Le Minaret' was exquisitely covered with a piece of gold lace. 'La Chemise de Rosine' was not only a scent but also a nightgown. His perfumes were such a success that he diversified Rosine, producing soaps, toilet waters and a whole range of cosmetics, including powder, make-up base, rouge, eye shadow and nail polish, again being the first couturier to link make-up to fashion (fig. 4). In 1945, when Marcel Rochas

organized an exhibition on the theme of perfumes, the exhibition was entitled *Hommage à Paul Poiret. Les parfums à travers la mode, 1765–1945.*

In the period 1911–13 Poiret took another giant step beyond his fellow couturiers with his fashion tours of Europe and the United States. They did not only introduce *haute couture* to fashionable women worldwide. While expanding his commercial empire on such a vast scale, he added a totally new dimension to the fashion trade. In the United States in 1913, in the words of Edith Woolman Chase, Poiret 'had received a rude jolt when he discovered that his models and name, as well as excellent copies of his dress labels were being freely hawked in America.'[3] Mrs Chase goes on to explain that Poiret was so appalled that on returning to Paris he contacted Philippe Ortiz of *Vogue*, asking him to consult the other couturiers with a view to seeking protection for original designs. This led to the establishment, in 1914, of Le Syndicat de la Défense de la Grande Couture Française, with Jacques Worth as vice-president and Poiret as president. Support came from the couturiers Paquin and the Callot Soeurs, and from the textile firms Rodier and Bianchini. Mrs Chase, the doyenne of *Vogue*, who knew both the French and American sides so well, pointed out that:

> ... *the American title, less sonorous, was nevertheless to the point: Protective Association of French Dressmakers, the announced purpose of which was 'to bring to an end the counterfeiting of labels and the illicit use of their names, thereby protecting the American public and honest importers from the false representations made by unscrupulous merchants and manufacturers'.*[4]

The First World War impeded the development of the Syndicat but this did not deter Poiret. In 1917 he was hoping to receive his discharge orders from the army and then to set up a company based in New York called 'Poiret Inc.'. Neither the discharge nor the company materialized but Poiret did sign 'the first contracts under license, ahead of Schiaparelli and Christian Dior'.[5]

In his autobiography, *My First Fifty Years*, Poiret points out the profit that could be derived from America provided the couturier showed the manufacturers that he was a member of a profession, had the right to pick and choose, and then signed a contract on his own terms:

> *This propensity of their manufacturers to enter into contact with famous men in order to be able to appropriate their names and profit by them is an American characteristic. How many of them made me magnificent offers, in order to be able to give the name of Poiret to their merchandise ... one amongst them ... who had set up as a manufacturer of shoes, in the neighbourhood of Lancaster, I think, made me a magnificent proposition: he would be authorized to use my name in his advertising and to print it on his luxury goods in return for which he would give me $16,000, a year.*[6]

After visiting his establishment and examining his goods Poiret refused this manufacturer his authorization. That the manufacturer wore a large-checked suit and had his jacket pocket stuffed with big cigars could not have helped. 'However I did sign contracts with manufacturers who made stockings, ladies' handbags, gloves, and especially, and now you will laugh, thread gloves!'[7]

In 1922 Poiret went to the United States again with models designed specially for American consumption and also with the express idea of establishing a system of royalties. According to Poiret's scheme, American manufacturers buying these models could copy them as often as they liked, but they would be charged for each copy. Again Poiret was prescient for 'thirty years later fashion houses adapted this system under the designation 'samples for exportation'.[8] It took all these years for the trail he started to blaze before the First World War to come full circle.

In the intervening years Poiret continued to further the profession of the *grand couturier*. In 1933, four years after his fashion house had disappeared, the department store Printemps asked him to create four collections per year for the sum of 20,000 francs per month:

> *It was a great first, if we remember that it was not until 8 June 1950 that Carven, Jean Dessès, Jacques Fath, Jean Paquin and Robert Piguet presented their collections at popular prices in the very same Printemps store.*[9]

Poiret worked for six months with Printemps. In 1933 he also received a commission from Liberty in London. The surviving designs bear the label 'Paul Poiret for Liberty'.[10]

In addition to his initiatives in the fashion trade, Poiret was also the first couturier to give lectures on women's dress. They deserve to be better known as they are of some significance in the history of fashion. His last visit to the United States, in 1927, was specifically to give lectures. On the role of the couturier he said:

> ... *we are not capricious despots who, when they awaken in the morning, decide to bring about some change in habits, to abolish the collar or make the sleeve swell. We are neither arbiters nor dictators ... Our role and our duty therefore consists in watching for the moment when She shall become tired of what She is wearing, so that then we may propose to Her, at just the right moment, something else that shall be in conformity with Her wishes and Her needs. Wherefore it is that I present myself before you armed with a pair of antennae, and not with a rod, and I do not speak to you as a master, but as a slave desirous of divining your secret thoughts.*[11]

Poiret recognized that fashion was continually evolving. For him, the couturier was not a dictator but a visionary.

He also thought fashionable American women, in spite of their far superior resources and riches when compared to their French counterparts, dressed in a very imitative and stereotyped way. His philosophy on how to dress is just as relevant today:

> ... *simply wear what becomes you. Look at yourselves in the mirror. Observe those tones that enhance the colours, and those that dim them. Adopt those which are favourable to you, and if blue suits you, don't think you ought to wear green because green is the fashion.*[12]

It was a theme he dwelt on in his fashion articles which should be considered as very much an adjunct to his lectures. In an article in *La Grande Revue*, of which he

51 '*La Dame en noir*' by Kees Van Dongen, 1924. The Poiret model wears a black-and-white outfit relieved by the elaborate embroidery on the bodice. A very fashionable garment at this date was the bolero jacket, a short jacket ending above the waistline and open in front. Poiret has given it long, full sleeves. The picture hat is plain with just a wide black ribbon band around the brim.

was particularly proud, he wrote:

> *There is only one principle of elegance,*
> *and the Romans summed it up in one*
> *word,* decorum. *That means what is*
> *suitable. Choose what is suitable,*
> *Madame, what is suitable to the hour,*
> *the circumstances, the temperature, the*
> *setting, the landscape, the place you*
> *live in, capital, spa, beach resort, or*
> *country. Choose with taste what is*
> *suitable to your character, for a gown,*
> *like a faithful portrait, reflects a state*
> *of mind, and there are gowns that sing*
> *of joy of living and others that are*
> *harbingers of tragedy.*[13]

Another of his views which holds true today was his firm belief that dress must have a relationship to contemporary life. In the May 1908 issue of *Vogue*, the Paris correspondent observed that:

> *... the fashionable figure is growing*
> *straighter and straighter. Here even the*
> *cab drivers and butcher boys have*
> *already become accustomed to seeing*
> *ladies stepping along sidewalks,*
> *holding closely in the hand the long*
> *skirt, which reveals plainly every line*
> *and curve from hip to ankle. The*
> *petticoat is obsolete, pre-historic.*[14]

By the time Poiret came to design his post-war fashions he had developed this idea further, drawing a sharp distinction between day dresses, which were more functional, and evening dresses which called for lavishness. The sagacious correspondent in *Vogue* alluded to another of Poiret's innovations which was so apropos of the twentieth century. Poiret's styles did not need layers and layers of undergarments. From now on all garments would be infinitely lighter and easier to wear.

In the catalogue to an exhibition of Poiret's paintings in 1937, Dufy wrote that 'you paint as you create clothes, with passion and elegance'.[15] Poiret, steeped in the history of art, particularly admired the artists Jacques-Louis David and Jean-Auguste-Dominique Ingres. They both put a great deal of emotion into their work and painted, with great refinement and taste, women often dressed in the neo-classical style. Poiret was, above all, an artist both with the brush and with clothes. It is best, however, to let him have the last word and to give his own assessment of his contribution to fashion:

> *... it is neither by restoring life to the*
> *new colour scheme, nor by launching*
> *new styles, that I think I rendered the*
> *greatest service to my epoch ... It was*
> *in my inspiration of artists, in my*
> *dressing of theatrical pieces, in my*
> *assimilation of and response to new*
> *needs, that I served the public of my*
> *day.*[16]

NOTES TO THE TEXT

Introduction

1 P. Poiret, *My First Fifty Years,* trs. Stephen Haden Guest, Victor Gollancz, 1931, p. 296.
2 Ibid., p. 104.
3 J. Robinson, *The Golden Age of Style*, Orbis, 1976, pp. 9–10; M. Ginsburg, V&A, Compton Press, Pitman Press, 1980, p. 11; E. W. Chase, *Always in Vogue*, Victor Gollancz, 1954, p. 94.
4 A. Mackrell, 'The Dress of the Parisian Élégantes with Special Reference to the *Journal des Dames et des Modes* from June 1797 until December 1799', unpublished MA thesis, Courtauld Institute of Art, University of London, 1977.
5 Poiret, op. cit., p. 63.
6 E. Bénézit, *Dictionnaire critique et documentaire des Peintres, Sculpteurs, Dessinateurs et Graveurs*, nouvelle édition, Librairie Gründ, Vol. 6, p. 590.
7 Robinson, op. cit., pp. 38 and 43.
8 P. White, *Poiret*, Studio Vista, 1973, p. 161.
9 Robinson, op. cit., p. 86; Arts Council of Great Britain, *Raoul Dufy 1877–1953*, London, 1983, p. 86.
10 B. Hillier, *The Style of the Century 1900–1980*, The Herbert Press, 1983, p. 81.
11 Ibid., p. 81.
12 Ibid., pp. 69–70.
13 Robinson, op. cit., p. 7.
14 Musée des Arts Décoratifs, *Les Années "25"*, Paris, 1966, Vol. I: *Art Déco*, pp. 46–7.
15 M. Battersby, *Art Deco Fashion: French Fashion Designers 1908–1925*, Academy Editions, 1984, p. 72; for the history of the *Gazette du Bon Ton* see Battersby, p. 72 and Chase, op. cit., pp. 93–7.
16 Erté, *Things I Remember: An Autobiography*, Peter Owen, 1975, p. 28; for the background on Erté entering Poiret's fashion house in January, 1913, see pp. 21–4.
17 Ibid., p. 37.
18 Poiret, op. cit., p. 26.
19 Erté, op. cit., p. 22.
20 F. Kennett, *Secrets of the Couturiers*, Exeter Books, 1984, p. 27.
21 C. Dior, *Christian Dior and I*, trs. Antonia Fraser, E. P. Dutton, 1957, p. 29.

Poiret et Nicole Groult. Maîtres de la Mode Art Déco, Paris, 1986, pp. 48 and 216, catalogue no. 23; C. Spencer, *Erté*, Studio Vista, 1970, p. 24.
2 J. Laver, *Taste and Fashion from the French Revolution until Today*, George G. Harrap, 1937, pp. 165–6.
3 White, op. cit., p. 29.
4 Poiret, op. cit., pp. 72–3.
5 Ibid., p. 25.
6 White, op. cit., p. 31.
7 Poiret, op. cit., p. 28.
8 Erté, op. cit., p. 26
9 D. Cooper, *The Rainbow Comes and Goes*, Rupert Hart-Davis, 1958, p. 61.
10 Ibid., p. 60.
11 V. Steele, *Fashion and Eroticism. Ideals of Feminine Beauty from the Victoria Era to the Jazz Age*, Oxford University Press, 1985, p. 226.
12 Poiret, op. cit., p. 97.
13 Bénézit, op. cit., Vol. 2, p. 245.
14 White, op. cit., p. 41.
15 Mackrell, op. cit., pp. 24–5.
16 G. Hubert, 'Josephine, a Discerning Collector of Sculpture', *Apollo*, Vol. CVI, No. 185 (new series), July 1977, pp. 34–43.
17 Y. Deslandres, 'Josephine and *La Mode*', *Apollo*, Vol. CVI, No. 185 (New Series), July 1977, pp. 46–7.
18 J. Bonaparte and P.-J. Redouté, *Roses for an Empress*, Sidgwick and Jackson, 1983.
19 Y. Deslandres, *Poiret*, Thames and Hudson, 1987, pp. 110–11.
20 White, op. cit., p. 64.
21 E. W. Chase, *Always in Vogue*, p. 120.
22 Poiret, op. cit., p. 73.
23 White, op. cit., pp. 71–2.
24 For a discussion of male fashions in feminine attire during the Directoire see Mackrell, op. cit., pp. 63–5.
25 Deslardres, *Poiret*, op. cit., p. 138
26 White, op. cit., pp. 24–5
27 Erté, op. cit., p. 25.
28 Mackrell, op. cit., pp. 27–8.
29 Metropolitan Museum of Art, *Diaghilev. Costumes and Designs of the Ballets Russes*, New York, 1978.

Chapter 1

1 Musée de la Mode et du Costume, *Paul*

Chapter 2

1 Hillier, op. cit., p. 70.

2 Poiret, op. cit., p. 178.
3 Hillier, op. cit., p. 75.
4 Cooper, op. cit., p. 61.
5 Poiret, op. cit., pp. 25–6.
6 Ibid., p. 36.
7 Ibid., p. 37.
8 Ibid., p. 65.
9 Ibid., p. 72.
10 Ibid., pp. 89–90.
11 Metropolitan Museum of Art, *Diaghilev. Costumes and Designs of the Ballets Russes*, 1978, unpaginated.
12 D. Vreeland, *Inventive Paris Clothes 1909–1939*, Thames and Hudson, 1977, p. 14.
13 Victoria and Albert Museum, *Fashion 1900–1939*, London, 1975, pp. 20, 59, No. A10.
14 Ibid., p. 59, No. A19.
15 Ibid., p. 59, No. A17.
16 Dior, op. cit., p. 30.
17 Metropolitan Museum of Art, op. cit.
18 J. L. Druesedow, 'In Style. Celebrating Fifty Years of the Costume Institute', *The Metropolitan Museum of Art Bulletin*, Vol. XLV, No. 2, Fall 1987, p. 53.
19 Poiret, op. cit., pp. 185–6, 188; for full description of the '1002nd Night', pp. 185–92.
20 J. Cocteau, *Paris Album 1900–1914*, trs. Margaret Crosland, W. H. Allen, 1956, p. 171.
21 Poiret, op. cit., p. 177.
22 White, op. cit., p. 83.
23 Ibid., p. 90.
24 Ibid., p. 90.
25 Victoria and Albert Museum, *Four Hundred Years of Fashion*, William Collins, 1984, p. 82.
26 Poiret, op. cit., p. 91.
27 Erté, op. cit., p. 25.
28 Ibid., p. 25.
29 Ibid., p. 26.
30 Ibid., pp. 25–6.
31 Poiret, op. cit., p. 79.
32 Musée de la Mode et du Costume, op. cit., p. 182.
33 Erté, op. cit., p. 28.
34 White, op. cit., p. 104.

Chapter 3

1 Y. Deslandres, *Poiret*, op. cit., p. 42.
2 Poiret, op. cit., p. 155.
3 Deslandres, *Poiret*, op. cit., p. 259; White, op. cit., pp. 117–18.
4 Poiret, op. cit., pp. 157–8.
5 Ibid., pp. 158–9.
6 White, op. cit., p. 120. For a colour

illustration of the 'Begonias' carpet see White, *op. cit.* p. 106.
7 Victoria and Albert Museum, *Four Hundred Years of Fashion*, p. 159, No. 142.
8 Deslandres, *Poiret*, p. 234.
9 White, op. cit., p. 127.
10 M. Battersby, *The Decorative Twenties*, Studio Vista, 1969, p. 85.
11 I. Duncan, *My Life*, Victor Gollancz, 1968, pp. 275–6.
12 White, op. cit., p. 66.
13 Duncan, op. cit., pp. 275–6.
14 Poiret, op. cit., pp. 160–1.
15 Ibid., p. 162.
16 London, Arts Council of Great Britain, *Raoul Dufy*, op. cit., p. 74.
17 Ibid., p. 74.
18 For a full account of the fête see Poiret, op. cit., pp. 197–201.
19 Deslandres, *Poiret*, p. 55.
20 Arts Council of Great Britain, op. cit., pp. 74, 178, catalogue no. 279.
21 Ibid., p. 178.
22 Ibid., p. 178.
23 *Encyclopédie des arts décoratifs et industriels modernes au XXème siècle*, Garland Publishing, 1977, Vol. IX Group de la Parure, Plate VII, *Robe du soir*, Mannequin Siégel and Stockmann.
24 Arts Council of Great Britain, op. cit., p. 87.
25 *Fashion in Paris from the 'Journal des Dames et des Modes' 1912–13*, Thames and Hudson, 1980, unpaginated.
26 Deslandres, *Poiret*, p. 155.
27 Arts Council of Great Britain, op. cit., p. 89.
28 White, op. cit., p. 47.
29 P. Poiret, *Art et Phynance*, Editions Lutetia, 1934, p. 111.

Chapter 4

1 Robinson, op. cit., p. 66; London, Victoria and Albert Museum, *Four Hundred Years of Fashion*, p. 83.
2 White, op. cit., p. 137.
3 Deslandres, *Poiret,* p. 261.
4 Ibid., p. 60.
5 White, op. cit., p. 148.
6. L. de Pougy, *My Blue Notebooks*, trs. Diana Athill, André Deutsch, 1979, p. 36.
7 Hillier, op. cit., p. 75.
8 Poiret, *My First Fifty Years*, op. cit., p. 229. For a full account of his visit to Morocco see pp. 229–39.
9 Deslandres, *Poiret,* op. cit., p. 151. See also p. 152.

10 Arts Council of Great Britain, op. cit., p. 82
11 Sotheby's, *Mode des Années 1840–1970. Collection Mary Vaudoyer*, Monaco 1987, p. 42, catalogue no. 147.
12 Ibid., p. 36, catalogue no. 121.
13 G. Howell, *In Vogue*, Penguin Books, 1978, p. 75.
14 de Pougy, op. cit., p. 206.
15 Howell, op. cit., p. 82.
16 White, op. cit., p. 157.
17 P. Byrde, *A Visual History of Costume: The Twentieth Century*, B. T. Batsford, 1986, p. 11.
18 Vreeland, op. cit., p. 32.
19 de Pougy, op. cit., pp. 67–8
20 Sotheby's, op. cit., p. 28, catalogue no. 86.
21 E. Ewing, *History of Twentieth-Century Fashion*, B. T. Batsford, 1974, p. 88.
22 London, Victoria and Albert Museum, *Four Hundred Years of Fashion*, p. 161.
23 Ibid., p. 84.
24 Deslandres, *Poiret*, pp. 152, 155.
25 P. Earnshaw, *A Dictionary of Lace*, Shire Publications, 1982, p. 40.
26 Deslandres, *Poiret*, op. cit., p. 217.
27 Laver, op. cit., p. 155.
28 Deslandres, *Poiret*, op. cit., p. 220.
29 Sotheby's, Monaco, op. cit., p. 2.
30 Ibid., p. 10, catalogue, no. 37.
31 Deslandres, *Poiret*, op. cit., p. 155.
32 London, Victoria and Albert Museum, *Four Hundred Years of Fashion*, p. 86.

Chapter 5
1 Arts Council of Great Britain, op. cit., pp. 16 and 38.
2 Ibid., p. 82.
3 Robinson, op. cit., pp. 60–1.
4 Arts Council of Great Britain, op. cit., p. 89.
5 Deslandres, *Poiret*, p. 78.
6 Musée Jacquemart-André, *Poiret, le magnifique*, Paris, 1974, p. 104, catalogue no. 462.

7 Ibid., p. 27, catalogue no. 63.
8 Bénézit, op. cit., Vol. 2, p. 319.
9 Chase, op. cit., p. 95.
10 White, op. cit., p. 139.
11 Deslandres, *Poiret*, op. cit., p. 303.
12 Musée Jacquemart-André, op. cit., p. 37, catalogue no. 130.
13 Ibid., p. 38, catalogue no. 131.
14 J.-E. Muller, *Fauvism*, trs. Shirley E. Jones, 1967, pp. 141–2.
15 Ibid., p. 146.
16 M. Ray, *Self-Portrait*, new edition, Bloomsbury Publishing, 1988, p. 101.
17 Ibid., p. 102.
18 Ibid., p. 104.
19 C. McDowell, *McDowell's Dictionary of Twentieth-Century Fashion*, revised edition, Frederick Muller, 1987, p. 287.
20 White, op. cit., p. 157.
21 Victoria and Albert Museum, *Fashion 1900–1939*, p. 25.

Conclusion
1 Deslandres, *Poiret*, p. 13.
2 Ibid., p. 16.
3 Chase, op. cit., p. 92; for Poiret's account see *My First Fifty Years*, op. cit., pp. 258–60.
4 Chase, op. cit., p. 93.
5 Deslandres, *Poiret*, op. cit., p. 22.
6 Poiret, *My First Fifty Years*, op. cit., p. 268.
7 Ibid., p. 269.
8 White, op. cit., p. 157.
9 Deslandres, *Poiret*, op. cit., pp. 22 and 24.
10 Ibid., p. 24; London, Victoria and Albert Museum, *Four Hundred Years of Fashion*, p. 162, catalogue no. 157.
11 Poiret, *My First Fifty Years*, p. 284.
12 Ibid., p. 297.
13 White, op. cit., p. 41.
14 Ibid., p. 41.
15 Ibid., p. 179.
16 Poiret, *My First Fifty Years*, p. 90.

GLOSSARY

Bouclé   from the French for buckle or curl. Used to describe a woven or knitted surface which has curls and knots.

Braid   a narrow band of various materials used as trimmings.

Brocade   a woven textile with a pattern of raised figures which are made by the threads of a different yarn or colour.

Cashmere   a very fine, luxurious wool. Originally woven entirely from the wool of the Tibetan goat. Later woven with a mixture of cotton, or cotton and wool woof. Cashmere shawls were originally made in Kashmir.

Charmeuse   a lustrous, silk-weave fabric.

Chiffon   a very soft, semi-transparent plain woven silk fabric.

Crêpe   a semi-transparent material with a crinkled surface.

Crêpe de Chine   a very soft China silk crêpe, plain or figured, woven from a silk warp and worsted weft.

Cross cut   cutting across the warp of the fabric to produce a line that is crosswise.

Faille   a silk with a ribbed weave.

Gauze   a very thin, sheer material woven in silk, linen or cotton.

Gold, cloth of   a fabric which is woven entirely of gold thread or of a mixture of gold thread and silk.

Grain   the direction of the warp and woof threads in a material. Can be lengthwise, crosswise or diagonal across the warp and woof.

Lamé   a material interwoven with gold or silver threads.

Lawn   a very fine, soft linen; also cotton in the twentieth century.

Muslin   a light, plain, openly woven cotton fabric. Also a general term for fine, soft cottons.

Net   a material of fine mesh.

Ombré   a colour which shades in tone.

Rayon   a manmade textile fibre made from cellulose.

Rib   a raised ridge in a material due to alternating wales (the weave or texture) in two different directions.

Satin   a silk fabric with a smooth, glossy surface on one side.

Satin ondoyant   a very light and supple satin. One of many high-quality materials used by Raoul Dufy and peculiar to the Bianchini-Férier silk firm in Lyons.

Shot   a fabric which is so woven that the colour differs according to the light.

Taffeta   a smooth, lustrous plain or patterned stiff silk fabric.

Tulle   a gossamer silk net. It was named after the French city of Tulle where the material was first made.

Twill   a fabric woven so as to have a surface of parallel ridges.

Velvet   a silk fabric with a pile produced by a pile warp, which, by the introduction of rods during weaving, is raised in loops. When the loops are cut, the material is called cut velvet.

BIBLIOGRAPHY

Albums

IRIBE, P., *Les robes de Paul Poiret racontées par Paul Iribe*, Société Générale d'Impression, 1908.

LEPAPE, G., *Les choses de Paul Poiret vues par Georges Lepape*, Maquet, 1911.

Memoirs

POIRET, P., *Art et Phynance*, Editions Lutetia, 1934. *My First Fifty Years*, trs. Stephen Haden Guest, Victor Gollancz, 1931.

Monographs

DESLANDRES, Y., *Poiret*, Thames and Hudson, 1987.

WHITE, P., *Poiret*, Studio Vista, 1973.

MEMOIRS AND DIARIES WITH REFERENCES TO POIRET

CHASE, E. W. and I., *Always in Vogue*, Victor Gollancz, 1954.

COCTEAU, J., *Paris Album 1900–1914*, trs. Margaret Crosland, W. H. Allen, 1956.

COOPER, D. *The Rainbow Comes and Goes*, Rupert Hart-Davis, 1958.

DIOR, C., *Christian Dior and I*, trs. Antonia Fraser, E. P. Dutton, 1957.

DUNCAN, I., *My Life*, Victor Gollancz, 1968.

ERTÉ, *Things I Remember: An Autobiography*, Peter Owen, 1975.

POUGY, L. DE, *My Blue Notebooks*, trs. Diana Athill, André Deutsch, 1979.

RAY, M., *Self-Portrait*, new edition, Bloomsbury Publishing, 1988.

FASHION MONOGRAPHS AND ARTICLES WITH REFERENCES TO POIRET

BATTERSBY, M., *Art Deco Fashion: French Fashion Designers 1908–1925*, Academy Editions, 1984.

The Decorative Twenties, Studio Vista, 1969.

BYRDE, P., *A Visual History of Costume: The Twentieth Century*, B. T. Batsford, 1986.

DRUESEDOW, J. L., 'In Style. Celebrating Fifty Years of the Costume Institute', *The Metropolitan Museum of Art Bulletin*, Vol. XLV, No. 2, Fall 1987.

EWING, E., *History of Twentieth-Century Fashion*, B. T. Batsford, 1974.

Fashion in Paris from the 'Journal des Dames et des Modes' 1912–13, Thames and Hudson, 1980.

GINSBURG, M., *An Introduction to Fashion Illustration*, V&A/Compton/Pitman, 1980.

HILLIER, B., *The Style of the Century 1900–1980*, The Herbert Press, 1983.

HOWELL, G., *In Vogue*, Penguin Books, 1978.

KENNETT, F., *Secrets of the Couturiers*, Exeter Books, 1984.

LAVER, J., *Taste and Fashion from the French Revolution until Today*, George G. Harrap, 1937.

MCDOWELL, C., *McDowell's Directory of Twentieth-Century Fashion*, new revised edition, Frederick Muller, 1987.

ROBINSON, J., *The Golden Age of Style*, Orbis Books, 1976.

SPENCER, C., *Erté*, Studio Vista, 1970.

STEELE, V., *Fashion and Eroticism. Ideals of Feminine Beauty from the Victorian Era to the Jazz Age*, Oxford University Press, 1985.

VREELAND, D., *Inventive Paris Clothes 1909–1939*, Thames and Hudson, 1977.

EXHIBITION CATALOGUES AND MUSEUM PUBLICATIONS

Encyclopédie des arts décoratifs et industriels modernes au XXème siècle, 12 vols., Garland Publishing, 1977, Vol. VI: 'Tissu et Papier'; Vol. IX: 'Group de la Parure (facsimiles of the Paris, *Exposition Internationale des Arts Décoratifs et Industriels Modernes*, 1925).

Arts Council of Great Britain, *Raoul Dufy 1877–1953*, London, 1983.

Metropolitan Museum of Art, *Diaghilev, Costumes and Designs of the Ballets Russes*, New York, 1978.

Musée de la Mode et du Costume, *Paul Poiret et Nicole Groult. Maîtres de la Mode Art Déco*, Paris, 1986.

Musée de l'Impression sur Etoffes, *Raoul Dufy, créateur d'étoffes*, Mulhouse, 1973.

Musée des Arts Décoratifs, *Les Années "25"*, 2 vols., Paris, 1966, Vol. 1: 'Art Déco'

Musée Jacquemart-André, *Poiret, le magnifique*, Paris, 1974.

Victoria and Albert Museum, *Fashion 1900–1939*, London, 1975.

Four Hundred Years of Fashion, 1984.

PERIODICALS

Gazette du Bon Ton, 1912–14, 1920–25.

Journal des Dames et des Modes, 1797–1839; 1912–14.

Les Modes, 1901–30.

Vogue, 1916–30.

SALE CATALOGUE

Sotheby's, Monaco, *Mode des Années 1840–1970. Collection Mary Vaudoyer*, 1987.

Museums with Poiret Collections

United Kingdom

London

Victoria and Albert Museum

Robe de minute. White silk damask evening dress, 1911. A two-piece, sleeveless straight cut tunic made for Mme Poiret to wear at the Berlin opera in 1911.

Emerald green satin opera cloak, c. 1911. Cut square and held in place at the low waist with a gilt braid loop. The dolman sleeves are of cloth of gold and a heavy gilt fringe trims the hem. Lined with purple chiffon.

Sorbet evening ensemble (skirt and tunic). Cream and black satin and pink chiffon with glass bead embroidery in pinks, mauves, and green with a fur edging, 1912. From Mme Poiret's collection.
Yellow and black mantle, c. 1913. Identical, separate panels of yellow wool lined in black silk wrapped across the body and held in place by a low, bow-trimmed belt.
Orange and fuschia mantle, c. 1913. Knee-length velvet kimono embroidered with a curvilinear pattern in gold thread and lined with golden yellow.

Samovar. Black evening dress, c. 1919. Semi-fitted V-necked sleeveless top embroidered in gold and black silk braid and a gathered skirt of black silk lace padded at the hips.
White satin evening dress, c. 1920. Single-shouldered dress with loosely fitting bodice; the skirt asymmetrically draped with a train at the back. A spray of red and white artificial flowers trims the shoulder, matching the scarlet chiffon facings of the dress.

Brique. Day dress, 1924. Fine orange worsted flecked with cream, trimmed with black and white rayon braid and tassels.
La flute. Black and white satin day dress, c. 1925. White satin long-waisted bodice with small square neck and long tight sleeves and a slightly flared black satin skirt. On the centre front is a flute motif embroidered in gold braid.
Tartan silk day dress, c. 1925–26. In pink, grey and black check. Straight-cut, low-waisted sleeveless bodice with square neck and black shoulder and hip yoke. The skirt panels are gathered on to the hip band.
Evening dress, 1933. Ivory satin, jade green silk velvet ribbons and diamanté buckles. One of a number of designs commissioned by Liberty's for their Model Gown Salon in London.

France

Paris

Musée de la Mode et du Costume

Robe Byzantine, 1904. Cloth of gold covered with pearls and Byzantine embroideries. Worn by the comtesse Greffulhe to the wedding of her daughter.

Révérend, 1905. Manteau-kimono in garnet-coloured cloth decorated with Chinese embroidery.
Evening dress, 1905. White taffeta with black velvet stripes. *Gigot* sleeves. White muslin trim on the bodice.
Evening coat, c. 1907. Chestnut-coloured cloth. Has a detachable hood. Inspired by the eighteenth century. For his autumn 1922 collection Poiret designed a similar one called *Varenne* in memory of Queen Marie-Antoinette.

Veste d'intérieur, c. 1907. Black net with long sleeves of pleated black muslin. Decorated with roses embroidered with threads of blue silk.
Afternoon dress, c. 1908. In *grenadine bleu* with a high-waistline, small kimono sleeves and with floral applications. This dress is attributed to Poiret on the basis of its similarity to dresses illustrated by Paul Iribe and also its similarity to the dress called *Toujours* in the collection of the Victoria and Albert Museum, London.

Maintenon, c. 1909. *Robe de cérémonie* in mauve taffeta with the bodice draped like a scarf.

Robe de petite cérémonie, 1910. A very finely pleated white cotton tunic with embroidery in a floral motif. The very high-waistline is held in place by a gold sash with tassels. Worn over a green silk skirt. A supreme example of Poiret's Directoire style.

Evening coat, *c.* 1911. In printed velvet with a design of stylised roses.

Garden party dress, *c.* 1911. In cream muslin, the bodice and bottom of the skirt decorated with gathered ribbons and applications of printed material representing roses.

Estivale, *c.* 1911. Dress of white crepon; the skirt has three flounces of red and green embroidery, the collar and belt of the high waistline and the cuffs of the long sleeves all in green.

Pelisse, 1911. Ribbed bottle-green velvet with a large grey collar and Brandenbourg buttons made of green velvet. Grey lining. This *pelisse* was created for Mme Poiret for the trip to Russia with Paul Poiret in October 1911.

Robe de cérémonie, *c.* 1912. Dress of blue damask garnished with gold lace opening out onto a *fourreau* of white satin and blue muslin edged with gold lace.

Afternoon dress, *c.* 1912. In embroidered cream tulle on a ground of rose satin.

Robe à jupe-culotte, 1913. In green *mousseline de soie* over black satin. Long sleeves, harem trousers.

Minaret, 1913. Evening ensemble. Harem trousers in violet muslin; tunic in fuschia muslin worn with a gold belt. A celebrated example of the fashion Poiret launched with his fête, the 1002nd Night in 1911.

Costumes worn by the Poirets for the *Festes de Bacchus*, 1912.

Linzeler, 1919. Evening *toilette* worn by Mme Poiret to a *soirée* at L'Oasis. A silver lamé dress which is backless and has a short *jupe à paniers*. The dress is worn over a *fourreau* also made in silver lamé.

Apollon, *c.* 1919. Coat in figured ottoman lined in orange silk crêpe.

Egyptienne, 1919–20. An evening dress of blue silk damask embellished with gold.

Aiglon, 1919–20. Short evening dress in gold lamé.

Evening dress, *c.* 1920. Short in front, long in back extending into a small square train. In gold *lamé* worn over a long tunic in green pleated *mousseline de soie*.

Robe à danser, 1921. Sleeveless dancing dress, in gold lamé embroidered with a floral motif. This dress is attributed to Poiret because of its similarity to some of his other creations, most notably his evening dress, *Tsin-Tsin*, 1921, which was photographed by Delphi. (Delphi's photograph is in the collection of the Archives de la Seine, Paris).

Tolède, 1921. Short-sleeved dress of crêpe Mogador in a shade of Venetian red. The skirt has a small flounce and the bodice has embroidery in red, gold and silver threads. The actress, Mlle Spinelly, wore this dress, among other Poiret creations, in the play, *Kiki.* In the same autumn-winter collection 1921 Poiret designed another version in yellow crêpe Mogador but without sleeves and flouncing.

Monaco coat, 1921. The top is in black wool embroidered with golden palmettes and the bottom is in black velvet.

Mexico, 1922. Afternoon jacket in chestnut-coloured wool with a white woollen collar. Buckskin fringes and decorations of metal roses and porcelain blue pearls. This 'Western style' jacket, worn by Philiberte de Flaugergue, although without a Poiret label, is one of the most original styles with which he experimented. He designed a *costume de cowboy* for the actress, Maud Loti, in 1925, which was reproduced in *L'Art et la Mode*, 14 March 1925.

Fedora, 1922. Evening cape in violet velvet lined in yellow velvet. It has two panels forming a stole, decorated at their extremities with coloured and gilded pearls.

Costumes de scène. Stage costumes created for Mlle Dumaine (1921) and Marthe Davelli (1923).

Toilette de récital, *c.* 1923. Long dress in the form of a chasuble with the skirt and short train in gold lamé and the bodice in black satin with floral motifs in yellow silk and gold lamé. Falling from the sleeves are two large panels of black crêpe georgette. This *toilette* was worn by the singer, Mme Washington-Stephens, at her recitals – the great panels served to amplify her dramatic gestures.

Sérail, 1923. Dress of white satin embroidered with geometrical motifs in gold thread. Long, very full skirt and pagoda sleeves. This dress with its ample skirt and pagoda sleeves is similar to the series of *robes bretonnes* that Poiret designed.

Sésostris, 1923. Evening coat in black crêpe-satin which has a landscape design in gold. Fur collar and fur trim on the train and sleeves. The back features a red velvet rectangular panel. Sésostris was the name of three very venerated Egyptian pharoahs. One of a series of costumes Poiret designed which evoked for him the splendours of Egypt.

Rodier, c. 1923. Coat in *kasha* (cashmere) with red motifs of Persian inspiration. This garment belonged to Mme Poiret.

Thamara, 1924. Long silk evening dress with large floral motifs in gold and silver lamé.

Corsage fauconnier, c. 1925. In chestnut-coloured crêpe with a lozenge pattern embroidered in gold thread. This garment was in the wardrobe of Germaine Boivin, a niece of Poiret.

Manteau de soirée, 1928. In red velours-chiffon. Pagoda sleeves trimmed with black fur. Poiret created this coat for the actresss, Constance Talmadge.

Ensemble, 1935. In black velvet consisting of a blouse, jacket and pantaloons. Created especially for the dancer, Nyota Inyoka.
Evening dress, c. 1935. Long dress made in chintz with a pattern of large floral bouquets on a black ground. *Décolleté* bodice, skirt draped behind evoking the bustle of the 1880s. Short sleeves made of black velvet.

Musée des Arts de la Mode

Cairo, 1907. Tunic in beige silk ottoman. High waistline and low neckline emphasized by red braid trim. Short sleeves completely embroidered with flowers in shades of gold, red and blue.

Hispahan, 1907. Three-quarter length coat in mustard-coloured cotton velvet embroidered with a Persian palm motif in the same colour.

Joséphine, 1907. Evening dress in ivory satin covered with a black tulle tunic which has gold braid trim around the bodice, short sleeves, high waist and hem. A rose is placed on the bodice. One of Poiret's most classic dresses, it was drawn by Paul Iribe in the album *Les robes de Paul Poiret racontées par Paul Iribe*, 1908, plate 10.
Evening dress, 1907. High-waisted, long-sleeved in mauve satin gauze and purple crêpe de Chine forming a striped pattern. The skirt opens at the left onto an underskirt in finely pleated mauve chiffon which has a gold braid trim and is held in place at the top by a row of buttons made in gold, red and green braid. This dress was drawn by Paul Iribe in the album *Les robes de Paul Poiret racontées par Paul Iribe*, 1908, plate 3.
Evening dress, 1907. Black tulle *fourreau* heavily embroidered with sequins, beads and paste studs. Short square train.
Evening coat, c. 1907. Full-length with Oriental floral designs in black and gold.
Evening dress, c. 1908. In yellow satin. Worn with a green chiffon tunic trimmed with mink and embroidered with Oriental motifs in green beads, silk and gold thread.

Evening dress, 1910. In black gauze over white satin. Embroidered with black and white beads forming geometrical patterns. Hem edged with black velvet.

Nénuphar, 1911. Lush purple-pink evening coat with a band of tulle embroidered with an interlacing pattern of silk thread in the same colour extending from the bottom of one sleeve to the other passing around the back of the neck.

Lavallière, 1911. Evening dress in ivory satin embroidered with crystal beads around the neckline. Purple lining which also serves as a facing at the neck, sleeves and hem. Wide belt draped low over the hips. Mme Poiret owned many versions of this dress in rainbow colours.

Fleurie, 1912. Soft white muslin summer dress with a tunic embroidered with small pink flowers and green leaves. The high-waistline is emphasized by pink braid and two large bronze buttons. A superb example of Poiret's Directoire style.

Mélodie, 1912. Afternoon dress in purple damask with long sleeves and the skirt slit in front. Worn with a purple velvet tunic having a cherry border, held in place at the neck by one large button, with a diagonal pocket sewn on the right side. The neck of the tunic is edged with a white frill.

Evening coat, 1912. In cherry-red uncut velvet, lined with purple crêpe de Chine. Edged with silver fringing. Fur collar embroidered with purple, cherry red and silver braid forming geometric patterns around a paste heart. Worn with the evening dress, *Eugénie*, 1907: red gauze embroidered with gold spots over red crêpe de Chine. Low neckline trimmed with red brocade spotted with gold and covered with a tulle modesty piece.

Evening coat, 1913. In orange silk covered with Oriental designs in gold brocade. Held in place by a row of gold buttons and green frog-fastenings. Fur trim on collar and sleeves. Lined in shot green taffeta.

Caucase, 1913. Chestnut-coloured silk divided skirt with side slits edged with gold braid.

Bretonne, 1919. Afternoon dress in black velvet. Front embroidered in red and white wool forming Breton-inspired patterns.

Malgré moi, 1919. Evening dress in black velvet. Two long panels cross at the back and tie in front. Gathered overskirt in black tulle with blue and green spangles forming stripes on a green ground.

Toute de suite, 1919. Afternoon dress in cherry red velvet. High turnover collar reveals a lining in printed cotton having china-blue flowers on a red ground. Sleeves and left front of the dress have slits which show the same lining.

Abbesse, c. 1920. Afternoon dress in purple velvet. High collar, full skirt, and wide sleeves which are turned back, showing a lining of cloth of gold.

Han Kéou, c. 1920. Evening dress. In reversible chestnut-brown silk with green Chinese designs.

Evening coat, 1920. In black uncut velvet with full sleeves and turned down collar held in place with black braid. Lined in apricot taffeta trimmed with gold lamé.

Mandchou, 1921. Gold lamé tunic.

Exotique, 1922. Afternoon dress in black crêpe de Chine printed with bold flowers and birds of paradise.

Evening coat-dress, 1922. In orange velvet trimmed with chestnut-coloured velvet and floral designs embroidered in silver thread.

Manège, 1922. Evening dress in black plush velvet. Sleeves lined in gold lamé. Bodice and back embroidered with gold thread and sequins.

Spi, 1922. Short-sleeved dress in green velvet embroidered with Oriental motifs in silver thread. Named for Mlle Spinelly.

Fils du ciel, 1923. Sleeveless dress in red velvet. Openings at the sides held in place by black satin ties. Neck and sides trimmed with gold braid and black satin bias.

Gondole, 1923. Grey satin dress. Deep V-neck with a softly pleated grey chiffon fill-in. Embroidery in grey silk trims the neckline, sleeves and hem.

Moroccan-inspired costumes, 1924.

Mistigri, 1925. Black velvet coat with full kimono sleeves. An interesting feature is the large rectangular bands in grey wool on the four sides of the coat which have intricate white embroidered borders.

Saltimbanque, 1925. Afternoon dress. Bodice in red leather and skirt in pleated black crêpe de Chine. Decorated with sequins and copper beads.

Dress in cherry-red plush velvet, 1925. Short sleeves with long flap extensions. The whole dress is embroidered with sumptuous patterns of metal and crystal beads.

A collection of the hats of Madeleine Panizon, c. 1920–28.

UNITED STATES OF AMERICA

New York

Costume Institute, Metropolitan Museum of Art

Theatre coat, 1912. Yellow and blue *charmeuse* trimmed with black velvet and silver lace.

Summer travelling coat, 1919–20. Ivory cashmere, straight cut with darker woven formal, floral pattern.
Black-ribbed daytime coat, 1919–20. A silk and wool mixture, trimmed with white leather cutwork, and a standing collar of white fur.
Two-piece afternoon dress, 1919–22. Made of faille, the top is a four-cornered handkerchief and the skirt is sarong-shaped. Red with a very wide navy blue hemline.
Wedding dress, 1925. An interesting feature are the lamé panels similar to those on a wedding dress which Poiret designed for Mlle Gaillard.

Museum of the City of New York

Hommage à Rousseau. Evening dress, c. 1910. Black and white silk top and skirt of silk voile. The lush floral and foliate pattern of embroidery on the skirt, consisting of pearls, rhinestones, and coloured beads, recalls the paintings of 'le douanier', Henri Rousseau.
Evening cloak, 1917. Purple satin lined with green. Trimmed with a fringe in purple silk and tassels.
Woollen promenade ensemble, c. 1919. A very tailored outfit consisting of a black-and-white check tunic and matching three-quarter-length coat, a long black skirt and a black scarf.
Afternoon ensemble, c. 1920. Dress, jacket and three-quarter-length coat. In wine-red duvetyn and floral printed silk in shades of blue and beige on a wine-red ground.
Afternoon coat, 1922. A combination of black satin and cartridge-pleated wool.
Evening dress, c. 1922. Bodice and side panels of black satin; long white satin skirt. A very wide band of embroidery in intricate geometric patterns gives definition to the waistline.
Evening dress, c. 1923. In pink satin, gathered to the left side, the low waistline held in place by an ornament made of silver and gold.

CHRONOLOGY

1879   Born 20 April in the rue des Deux-Ecus, Paris, the son of a cloth merchant.

1891   Attended the Ecole Massillon.

1896   Earned Baccalauréat. Apprenticed by his father to an umbrella maker.

1898   Visited Madame Chéruit, *directrice* of La Maison Raudnitz. She bought a dozen of his dress designs at 20 francs each.

1898–   Apprenticeship with the *grand*
1900   *couturier*, Jacques Doucet.

1901   Joined La Maison Worth.

1903   Opened his own fashion house at 5 rue Auber, Paris.

1905   Married Denise Boulet.
Toured museums of Europe.

1906   Moved his fashion house to 37 rue Pasquier, Paris.

1908   First album: *Les robes de Paul Poiret racontées par Paul Iribe.*

1909   Moved his fashion house to the Hôtel d'Antin, avenue d'Antin.
Trip to London to see the Oriental turbans at the South Kensington Museum (Victoria and Albert Museum).
Article entitled 'Les Opinions de Monsieur Pétrone' in May issue of *La Grande Revue.*
Birth of his daughter, Rosine.

1911   Second album: *Les choses de Paul Poiret vues par Georges Lepape.*
Fashion tour of European capitals, including Frankfurt, Berlin, Warsaw, Moscow, St Petersburg, Budapest, Vienna, Munich, Bucharest.
Birth of his second daugher, Martine.
Established Martine school and shop, devoted to the decorative arts; Rosine, the very first house of perfume; Colin, a paper and packaging workshop; the Petite Usine or 'Little Factory' for textile printing with Raoul Dufy.
Fête of the '1002nd Night'.

1912   'Les Festes de Bacchus'.
Mediterranean cruise with Madame Poiret and a group of artists, visiting Italy, Spain and North Africa.
Birth of his son, Colin.

1913   Fashion tour of the USA. Saw copies of his dress designs and recognized the need for copyright legislation. Helped set up (in 1914) Le Syndicat de Défense de la Grande Couture Française et des Industries s'y Rattachant. (The First World War impeded its development and it was not until the 1950s that legislation was finally passed.)

1914   First World War. Served as a tailor in the
–18   army.

1918   Visited Morocco.

1919   Relaunched his fashion house.
Opened L'Oasis.

1920   Lecture 'In Defence of Fashion' at the Autumn Salon.

1922   Second fashion tour of the USA.

1924   Fashion house placed in the hands of a Board of Directors.

1925   Participated in the *Exposition des Arts Décoratifs et Industriels Modernes*, Paris.
Moved his fashion house to 1 Rond-Point des Champs Elysées, Paris.
Owing to severe financial difficulties Poirot sold his collection of paintings at a public auction at the Hôtel Drouot, Paris.

1926   Martine and Rosine companies sold.

1927   Final tour of the USA, giving lectures on dress. Wrote article entitled 'Will Skirts Disappear?' for *The Forum*.
Brought out album entitled *Pan*, designed to advertise French luxury products.

1928   Divorced.

1929   Closure of his fashion house.

1930   Wrote his memoirs. Spent six months of
–34   1933 creating designs for the department store Printemps. Published titles of his memoirs: *En habillant l'époque*, 1930 (translated as *My First Fifty Years*, 1931); *Revenez-y*, 1932; *Art et Phynance*, 1934.

1944   Spent last years painting.
Exhibition of his paintings at the Galerie Charpentier, Paris.
Died in Paris on 28 April.

INDEX

Note: Figures in italic type refer to pages on which illustrations appear.